The Poesten Kill

The Poesten Kill

WATERFALLS TO WATERWORKS
IN THE CAPITAL DISTRICT

JOHN WARREN

Charleston ┤├ London

THE
History
PRESS

Published by The History Press
Charleston, SC 29403
www.historypress.net

Copyright © 2009 by John Warren
All rights reserved

First published 2009

Manufactured in the United States

ISBN 978.1.59629.633.6

Library of Congress Cataloging-in-Publication Data

Warren, John, 1967-
The Poesten Kill : waterfalls to waterworks in the capital district / John Warren.
p. cm.
Includes bibliographical references.
ISBN 978-1-59629-633-6
1. Poesten Kill Region (N.Y.)--History. 2. Rensselaer County (N.Y.)--History,
Local. I. Title.
F127.R3W37 2009
974.7'41--dc22
2009007038

For Estelle Nelson, grandmother and gardener,
who first introduced me to history.

CONTENTS

Preface

Those familiar with the area may wonder why I've used the older spelling of Poesten Kill. I've done so in order that we might not forget the stream's nearly 350-year-long history and because its size and power hardly warrant the inferior appellation *creek*—the Dutch word *kill* just seems right. Besides, calling the waterway Poestenkill Creek is like calling it Poesten Creek Creek. For similar reasons, when discussing early Dutch settlers I have used the older spellings of Dutch names, such as van der Heyden, rather then the anglicized Vanderheyden, at least until the latter spelling was firmly established. I used the most common spellings for various geographic features and place names, with the exception of the preference of the older spelling Hoosac over Hoosic (both are correct), or Hoosick.

Acknowledgements

Although errors and omissions here are entirely my own, I'm grateful to the many historians whose work I've drawn from, notably those of the Poesten Kill's industrial history: Thomas Phelan, P. Thomas Carroll, Tammis Groft and labor historian Gerald Zahavi. Able local historians whose work was required reading included Florence Hill, Linda Sagendorf, Sharon Martin Zenkel and nineteenth-century chroniclers Arthur J. Weise, Nathaniel B. Sylvester and George Baker Anderson. Recent work on the early colonial and contact period by James Bradley, Shirley Dunn, Janny Venema, Paul Huey, Stefan Bielinski and Hartgen Archaeological Associates has been immeasurably helpful.

Additional source material was also drawn from census records, local and national newspapers, local directories and maps from my personal collection, the Troy Public Library, the New York State Library, the State University of New York at Albany Library, the Schenectady Public Library and the New York Public Library. A selected bibliography follows the text.

A debt of personal thanks is owed to Poestenkill Town Historian Linda Sagendorf for her cheerful and timely helpfulness. The History Press's Jonathan Simcosky and Kate Pluhar ably shepherded this project. My partner Shannon Houlihan provided support and encouragement, including hot meals, warm coffee and a willing ear. J.K. helped keep the fire going.

I can be contacted at http://poestenkill.blogspot.com, where discussion, comments and corrections are welcome.

INTRODUCTION

On the Hudson River along upstate New York's eastern border, within the natural boundaries of river and mountains, lies the rough rectangle of Rensselaer County. It is literally cut in half by the Poesten Kill, a powerful stream that scours its way downhill from 1,600 feet high in the Petersburg Mountains to the sea-level flats of the Hudson River. The Poesten Kill splits the county across the middle into two pieces of roughly equal size, north and south. It tumbles off the mountains, meanders across a ten-mile-wide plateau and then falls abruptly through a series of steep gorges to settle into the Hudson River flood plain.

Although frequently hidden now behind modern development and historic ruins, the Poesten Kill's geologic wonders are impressive. As it descends, the kill cuts through layers of rock, shale and silt and emerges from forested mountains, winds through rolling farmland, falls over steep cliffs and slides into the tidal Hudson. There are five major natural waterfalls on the Poesten Kill. They include Poesten Kill High Falls (Mount Ida Falls) in Troy, Barberville Falls east of Poestenkill Village and three falls in the town of Brunswick: the falls at Eagle Mills, Fred's Falls in Cropseyville (on the Poesten Kill's largest tributary, the Quacken Kill) and Buttermilk Falls. There have been dozens of places where the power of the Poesten Kill was captured by dams, raceways, water wheels and turbines, including a hydroelectric plant at the High Falls in Troy. In 1992, a small hydro plant was proposed at Barberville, but local opposition to the project, which would have despoiled the natural

Ruins of a mill at the top of Barberville Falls. The stones shown here were later rebuilt to provide a popular lookout for visitors to the falls, now owned by the Nature Conservancy. A small hydroelectric plant was proposed on the opposite bank in 1992. *Courtesy Poestenkill Historical Society.*

scenery of the Nature Conservancy–owned falls, ended it in its infancy.

The waters of the Poesten Kill, with the addition of the substantial waters of the Quacken Kill, drain into the Hudson River in a relentless journey to the Atlantic at New York Harbor. Its cavernous gorges and spectacular falls have served as inspiration to generations of artists and nature lovers. Atop Mount Ida is the city of Troy's Prospect Park, one of several natural areas protected by local governments and organizations, including Dyken Pond, Belden Pond and Barberville Falls. Nineteenth-century geologists once celebrated the Logan Fault, a thrust of older Cambrian rock that lies on top of newer Ordovician and runs from Canada to Alabama. It's now called the Emmons Thrust after Ebenezer Emmons, who graduated in the first class at Rensselaer Polytechnic Institute (RPI).

Introduction

The Poesten Kill has been home to American Indians who hunted, gathered, fished and farmed along its shores; frontier Dutch farmers and traders; colonial tradesmen, merchants, millers and lumbermen; and nineteenth-century iron, steel, textile and paper workers. Dutch, English, Irish, German, French and Italian immigrants, and others, have lived along its length. Its mouth at the Hudson was the first truly European *frontier* settlement beyond the walls of Fort Orange (what is now Albany). It was initially hoped that Greenbush would be the primary town for both sides of the Hudson, but the political reality of competing stakeholders (notably the Dutch West India Company and the Patroon Kiliaen van Rensselaer) made this impossible. One of the defining factors was that private settlers preferred citizenship at Beverwijck outside the gates of Fort Orange over the indentured servitude of the patroon's feudal lands. So it was that Greenbush was settled before the Poesten Kill, but with its close association to Albany by ferry, it could hardly be described as frontier; the city of Rensselaer was once known as East Albany.

On the west side of the Hudson, flooding and terrain generally restricted the early development of farms and major industry. Four miles north of Fort Orange, the patroon established a farm once called *de Vlackte* (the Flatts), later known as West Troy and today Watervliet. The small community there was considerably closer to the fort than those on the Poesten Kill and much more connected to life there. To the north of the Poesten Kill, settlement was constrained where the Mohawk River meets the Hudson by enormous cliffs and the falls of Cohoes, which made river travel above Troy impossible. The Piscawan Kill lay to the north, but at its mouth was a Mohican community, so it was settled only later by Europeans. The Piscawan Kill provided plenty of room for Dutch *bouweries* (farms) and served most of the city's water needs until about 1900, but it was not nearly powerful enough for major industry. Farther north, the Hoosac River held a substantial place in Native American and colonial history, but it was settled by Europeans much later than the Poesten Kill and faded in prominence during the latter part of the Industrial Revolution. The Wynants Kill, closer to the Poesten Kill, was settled at about the same time. Its short and ragged drop made it suitable for water power but not for farms and homes. Unlike its neighbor to the north, where the Wynants Kill enters the Hudson, there is only a small flood plain, not wide enough for substantial settlement. The banks of the Wynants Kill also found prominence during the Industrial Revolution but faded thereafter and have never served as an urban neighborhood, as the lower Poesten Kill has.

So the Poesten Kill was a frontier outpost that seemingly had it all: a large, flat, farmable flood plain and a potent source of water power, as well as room to grow. From the mouth of the Poesten Kill, Manhattan Island, the Atlantic seaboard, Lake Champlain, Montreal, the St. Lawrence River, the Mohawk River, the Great Lakes, the Hoosac River and New England were all within reach—even in prehistoric times. The markets at Albany, New York and later Troy in particular are crucial to understanding the development along the Poesten Kill.

The force of the water in the Poesten Kill helped drive the early development of Troy, once one of America's most important nineteenth-century industrial cities. The Poesten Kill's waters were harnessed for the American Industrial Revolution that built the golden age of American industry, trade and commerce; its banks afterward stood witness to industrial abandonment and urban decline. Mills established along the Poesten and Quacken Kills sent their goods—mostly grain, farm produce, wool, cotton and iron products, but also a variety of other consumer goods—to the markets at Troy and beyond. For instance, in the 1870s Poestenkill Village was home to saw- and gristmills, a cotton batten factory, a flax mill and a shirt factory. At the same time, mills along the Quacken Kill produced twine and carpet warp, paper, brush handles, cotton batten and carded and fulled wool, including cashmere, flannel and yarn. At Eagle Mills, there were saw- and gristmills, two iron foundries producing hoes and other farm tools and, nearby, three shirt factories.

At the head of Hudson River navigation, the mouth of the Poesten Kill was located at the eastern end of the Erie Canal and the southern end of the Champlain canal. It was also an important center of the very early Rensselaer & Saratoga and later Troy &

The bridge at Barberville just before the kill reaches the falls was the site of frequent destructive floods. This part of the Poesten Kill has changed little since 1800, but it no longer provides forest products for markets in Troy. *Courtesy Poestenkill Historical Society.*

Greenbush and New York Central Railroads. The Poesten Kill was home to the first paper factory in northern New York, and for many years Troy rivaled Pittsburgh in iron and steel production. What really made life along the Poesten Kill so unique, however, was the diversity of products made there. Unlike other eastern urban areas, the Poesten Kill was home to producers of agriculture and forest products along with feed, flour, paper, plaster, paint, textiles, iron and steel products like stoves, valves and wire—a substantial variety of consumer goods used along the kill and in the world beyond.

THE LAY OF THE LAND

The Poesten Kill begins with springs and streams that feed Dyken Pond, twenty miles east of the Hudson in the Petersburg Mountains. The pond is located near the corner of the towns of Poestenkill, Grafton and Berlin and some seven miles from where New York, Vermont and Massachusetts come together. As late as the turn of the last century, this pond was still known as "dyking pond," an indication of its long history. The modern dam enlarged the pond to the size of a small lake when it was built in 1902 by Manning Paper Company to regulate the water power and reduce the threat of flooding. The company donated the pond and some surrounding acres to Rensselaer County in 1973, and it is now home to the New York State Department of Conservation's Dyken Pond Environmental Education Center.

From Dyken Pond the Poesten Kill gathers strength as it comes off the Petersburg Mountains. It tumbles south through the eastern end of the town of Berlin and then turns west through the hamlet of East Poestenkill (once called Columbia). Winding its way through the eastern part of the town of Poestenkill, it picks up water from a dozen smaller streams to create the rush that makes the ninety-two-foot drop at Barberville Falls and brings the kill to the broad swath of the Rensselaer Plateau. Here the first substantial village along its course, Poestenkill, was settled. Still some seven miles from the Hudson, the kill leaves Poestenkill Village and turns north-northwest, where it's joined by the waters of the Newfoundland Creek as it meanders through rolling farmland.

The Lay of the Land

Below the Poestenkill Village, the kill turns northwest and meanders through rolling farmland, once some of the earliest farms established in the towns of Poestenkill and Brunswick. *Courtesy Poestenkill Historical Society.*

Near the Brunswick-Poestenkill town line, the Poesten Kill meets the waters of the Quacken Kill as it turns north again toward its second substantial village, Eagle Mills (formerly Millville). As Troy was growing to the east, a dam was built on the Quacken Kill to divert water into the city's water system from four ponds in the town of Grafton: Long, Second, Mill and Shaver. Dams built on these ponds controlled the flow of water down the Quacken Kill to the Eagle Mills diverting dam, where it was taken by a cast-iron main to the Brunswick Reservoir. In 1938, another sixteen-inch main was installed from the diverting dam and along Pinewoods Avenue to connect with the city system. The diverting dam reduced the flow of water in the Quacken and Poesten Kills and may have hastened the abandonment of some of the mills along both.

Leaving Eagle Mills, the Poesten Kill turns west again against steep canyons before settling down into a fairly straight and flat course where Sweet Milk Creek enters from the north on its way to the Country Club of Troy. The club was established in 1927, nestled into a large bend in the kill. It's the only private club in

In the 1860s and until it was replaced by this stone bridge in the late 1880s, the Pawling Avenue Bridge was known as the "Red Bridge." A bridge stood near here at the Fonda farm before the American Revolution. *Courtesy Troy Public Library.*

Rensselaer County and includes a clubhouse that overlooks the Poesten Kill designed by New York City architect Pliny Rogers. The golf course was designed by the first American golfer to win the British Amateur Championship, Walter J. Travis. The club was built on 170 acres of undeveloped land and adjacent farmland just before a series of three hairpin turns in the kill near the end of Cole Lane, off Pinewoods Avenue. There was an early paint mill here where workers mined shale from the ledges of the Poesten Kill and loaded them into scows to be floated to the mill and ground for red paint. The ruins of the mill's dam were still visible in the 1930s, but today the kill continues to flow toward city-owned Belden Pond, once part of the larger Ida Lake, a former millpond and the location of an early bleach works.

After passing under the bridge at Pawling Avenue (one of the oldest across the kill), the Poesten Kill plunges over the High Falls and cuts an enormous gorge through the southeast side of Mount

The Lay of the Land

Ida, the source of numerous destructive landslides in the past. At the base of Mount Ida, the Poesten Kill once meandered but today settles into an urban canal. The Hudson River now runs a straight course at the mouth of the Poesten Kill, but it once also meandered to form islands, large and small, spiral shoals and long, thin, sandbars that came and went with the changes in the river. Tidal flats lined the banks, some flooding annually, to provide rich soil for the summertime crops that the people living along the river planted. Before being harnessed for the Industrial Revolution, the Poesten Kill's meandering extended the flats at its mouth where the local Mohican, and later Europeans, settled.

NATURAL BEAUTY AND HEALING WATERS

An important aspect of the Poesten Kill is its natural beauty. Before the early 1800s, the wild areas along the Poesten Kill were generally considered an obstacle to overcome, a waste of land or the home of dangerous animals (and people), not a place of refuge or beauty. Still, a number of locals and some travelers passing through the area partook in the beauty and serenity the Poesten Kill then afforded, in particular its cool, clean water. In the late 1700s, there were a number of active springs on or near the Poesten Kill that drew visitors. Initially, most of those living near the lower Poesten Kill got fresh drinking water from the spring on Hollow Road (now Spring Avenue) on the farm of Stephen J. Schuyler. In 1800, the patroon (then Stephen van Rensselaer, the eighth and second to last patroon of Rensselaerswyck) conveyed the rights to the spring to Dr. Israel Clark of West Windsor, New Jersey, who built a small reservoir and collected payments for use of the water. In 1812, the Earthen Conduit Company of Troy was given the rights to pipe the water into Troy, and two years later it dropped the "earthen" and used new iron pipes. In 1833, the water supply was shifted to the Piscawen Kill, where a series of reservoirs was built.

The hamlet of Poestenkill also had a spring that became a center of sorts for those looking to "take the waters," and Dr. Matthew Moody erected several bathhouses at the base of Poole Hill just east of the bridge before 1812. The importance of this spa was demonstrated by the naming of the street leading to them "Bath

Natural Beauty and Healing Waters

Street," although long after the spring disappeared, this street became "The Back Street" and finally "Back Street." The spring must have attracted a large number of visitors because visitors remarked that boardinghouses for the ill were found around town. The spring waters were used to relieve neuralgia or erysipelas, an inflammatory skin condition, and Dr. Moody also offered a remedy to be taken along with the mineral baths:

8 oz. Spirit of Nitre	½ oz. Oil of Oreganum
1 oz. gum camphor	½ oz. Spirit of Salammonia
1 oz. Oil of Turpentine	12 oz. alcohol
1 large spoonful laudanum	

To be applied with the hand, well rubbed on. Good for man and beast.

In 1814, one or more millponds upstream of the hamlet burst after a heavy two-day rain, and the flood swept away the spring and several buildings, including a tannery operated by John Beals, seven other buildings, the boardinghouses and several bathhouses. One of the bathhouses ended up near a farm downstream and was used as a summer kitchen; another was carried by the flood to a home, where it was connected and used as a bedroom. The flood changed the look of Poestenkill hamlet as many of the older Colonial-style dwellings were destroyed and were replaced with Federal and Greek Revival styles.

It is likely that the early farmers, millers, colliers, lumberers and teamsters helped spread the word of the springs and waterfalls on the Poesten Kill, but it was the early artists and travelers whose records remain. One of the first depictions of the beauties of the Poesten Kill High Falls was an engraving made in Paris in 1817. As the 1800s wore on, changing attitudes about nature, combined with regional guides and maps, led to an increase in American travel for travel's sake. The coming of regular stagecoach and later railroad service to Troy meant more visitors to the natural wonders along the Poesten Kill. Guidebooks in the 1820s remarked on the natural beauty and often noted the location of Mount Ida and the falls.

Water courses through the village of Poestenkill. The first recorded flood there occurred in 1814, when one or more millponds upstream of the hamlet burst after a heavy two-day rain. *Courtesy Poestenkill Historical Society.*

Mount Ida was noted for its scenic views, and in 1832 one visitor wrote that "every house and store may be seen with perfect distinctness, while the eye is likewise gratified by a very extensive view north and south embracing the nine locks at the junction of the western and northern canals…two streams. Which afford an immense quantity of water power, empty into the Hudson…and one of them rolls down a beautiful cascade…which is frequently visited as an object of curiosity." In July 1837, the English naval officer and novelist Captain Frederick Marryat visited Troy and climbed Mount Ida. "I remained two hours perched upon the top of the mountain," he wrote. "I should have not have staid so long, perhaps, had they not brought me a basket of cherries, so that I could gratify more senses than one." The British artist W.H. Bartlett climbed Mount Ida and sketched a view of Troy that was published in London in *American Scenery* in 1840. In the 1850s, other views were issued from the same vantage point. The editor of the 1851 *Wilson's Hudson River Guide* remarked favorably on the beauty of the Poesten Kill gorge, describing it as "very narrow and lined with almost perpendicular rocks overhung with trees and shrubs of various hues…the scenery is wild, picturesque and beautiful."

Natural Beauty and Healing Waters

This somewhat fanciful version of British artist's W.H. Bartlett's sketch *View from Mount Ida* was one of many views from the same vantage point published in the nineteenth century. Bartlett's original sketch was published in London in *American Scenery* in 1840. *Courtesy Troy Public Library.*

Throughout the 1800s, visitors brought picnics to the Poesten Kill's most popular wild places: the base of the High Falls, the top of Mount Ida and the Buttermilk and Barberville Falls. In 1878, RPI student Rodney Kight wrote to his mother in Pennsylvania about a visit to the Poesten Kill:

> *As the weather was fine, we again took the streetcar up Mount Ida and stood atop the northern bank of the gorge. The waters are powerful there, and quite awhile ago Mister Marshall drilled a long sluice through the solid rock in order to drive his mill. One can still see the tunnel from above. My chums thought it would be grand to throw my hat into the falls below (I am the*

The ninety-two-foot drop at Barberville Falls has been a popular picnic and swimming spot for centuries. There are four other major natural waterfalls on the Poesten Kill: Poesten Kill High Falls, Eagle Mills, Fred's Falls and Buttermilk Falls. *Courtesy Poestenkill Historical Society.*

Natural Beauty and Healing Waters

underclassman!). When we finally descended the mount, they attempted to douse me with water. I know it's all in good fun. We bathed in the gorge for most of the day and walked back to the club soaked to save our fare.

In 1903, the City of Troy purchased the Warren and Vail properties on the top of Ida Hill, and Garnett D. Baltimore, RPI's first black graduate, designed Prospect Park. He had previously (in 1897) designed the now much neglected but then picturesque two-hundred-acre Forest Park Cemetery on Pinewoods Avenue. Prospect Park's winding roads once included fountains, a band shell, playgrounds, flower gardens, tennis courts and a public pool. The former residences of the Warren and Vail families were turned into a museum and a casino and towers and lookouts provided lengthy views along the Hudson below. Areas were designated for croquet and ball games, but no games were permitted in other areas of the park, and no games whatsoever could be played on Sundays. Dogs

Friends of Prospect Park and the Mount Ida Preservation Society have been slowly working to bring the gorge, pond and park back to their old grandeur. Ida Lake, seen in this view toward Route 2, was once a popular ice-skating spot. *Courtesy Troy Public Library.*

27

were required to be leashed and fires and alcohol were banned, as were lying "in indecent positions," telling fortunes, playing games of chance, fishing, bathing and disturbing animals, fish or birds.

In the 1960s, '70s and '80s, the Poesten Kill gorge, Prospect Park, Mount Ida Cemetery and Belden Pond all fell into disrepair. Many of the remaining buildings (particularly in the park) were either destroyed by fire or torn down; cast-iron railings that once graced the area were removed and the natural beauty was all but abandoned to trash, industrial waste and graffiti. In 1972, the Hudson Mohawk Industrial Gateway was established to advocate for the historic preservation and adaptive reuse of the area's industrial heritage, but by then it was largely too late. In the 1980s, an effort was made to clean up the gorge, but it failed when vandals destroyed new split-rail fences and signage. Another more successful effort was made in the gorge and at Prospect Park and Belden Pond in the late 1990s. Today, volunteer organizations such as the Friends of Prospect Park and the Mount Ida Preservation Society have been slowly working to bring the gorge, pond and park back to their old grandeur.

THE MOHICAN

A Bountiful Poesten Kill

T here were many Indian villages near the mouth of the Poesten Kill when the first Europeans arrived there, and the Mohican had already named many of the surrounding areas. One substantial community, located at the confluence of the Mohawk and Hudson, was known as Monemin's Castle after the Mohican chief killed in battle with the Mohawk in 1626. This village was the northern limit of Killian van Rensselaer's lands on the Hudson's west side, and by 1651, the people of Monemin's Castle had moved to the north of Greenbush. A Mohican named Dickop, considered a friend of the Dutch, lived on the south side of the Wynants Kill. Another large and politically important community was located in Schodack. These communities suffered from increasing tensions between the Mohican, Mohawk and Europeans over trade and land and were forced to migrate eastward by the time of the French and Indian War.

The most significant native community for the first settlers of the Poesten Kill in the mid-1640s was Unuwat's Castle. It was a palisaded village located just north of the Poesten Kill on the north side of the Piscawan Kill near what is now 101st Street. Little is known about Unuwat; the name does not appear on the many purchase agreements between the Mohican and Dutch, leading some to believe that it may be descriptive. Indian oral tradition records the presence of a crystal outcropping, known in later years as "diamond rock," that was located near Unuwat's Castle. Native inhabitants mined local flint for use as tools and buried their dead nearby at what is now the Waterford Bridge. Some Mohican lived very near to Europeans—these included those at Unuwat's Castle and in Greenbush.

Near Unuwat's Castle and to its north lay a woodland called *Passquassick* and above that a level and fertile spot known as *Tascamcatick*—these would become Lansingburgh. South of Unuwat's Castle between the Piscawan Kill and the Poesten Kill was *Paanpaach*, prime Hudson River bottomland also known as the "great meadow." Here the Mohican had planted crops, and the land was remembered as the "corn land of the Indians" in 1720. Woodlands east of *Paanpaach* were conveyed to Andries Albertse Bratt in 1684 by two Mohican, Annape (also spelled Alnape in the same deed) and Amahamett.

We know from evidence excavated at the Goldkrest Site on the east bank of the Hudson near Papscanee Island, and from early documents and narratives, that the Mohican lived in small communities and moved frequently between the Hudson flats and tributaries on the higher ground above. Most of the sites contained only a few buildings and covered about half an acre but had complex storage, cooking and food processing infrastructure, including a range of hearths, racks and pits for storage and buildings made of lashed bent poles. Some were small domed structures covered with reeds and rushes called *wetu* (wigwam); others were larger, elongated longhouses covered with bark. The Goldkrest Site revealed clay pots, stone tools, nuts, herbs, berries, freshwater mussels, local fish and local wildlife.

Visitors to the area throughout the 1600s noted the abundance of wild geese and turkeys, teal, pigeons, white-tailed deer, moose, beavers, otters; large quantities of grapes, plums, walnuts and hazelnuts; and fields planted in corn, beans and squash. The Poesten Kill is also a spawning ground for Hudson River fish, including shad, alewife and blueback herring. Caught with weirs and nets, they provided quick meals and abundant baitfish for larger catches of sturgeon, bass and salmon found in the Hudson (these were also taken by spear). In 1825, a seine net on the Hudson caught twenty-nine striped bass, weighing 245 pounds in all; two of the fish were said to have weighed an aggregate of 52 pounds. Before decades of pollution ravaged the Hudson and the lower Poesten Kill, the area had a closer ecological connection to the sea. In 1647, for instance, several whales accidently beached themselves near the mouth of the Poesten Kill (almost 160 miles from the New York Harbor), creating a terrible stench and leaving the Hudson "oily for three weeks."

THE DUTCH

Van Rensselaer's East Manor

Europeans settlement of the area began across the Hudson, ten miles south of the Poesten Kill, after the construction of Fort Orange by the Dutch in 1624. Beginning in 1630, land extending more than twenty miles around the fort on both sides of the river was negotiated from the Mohican for merchant Kiliaen van Rensselaer's feudal manor, Rensselaerswyck. The area where Troy now stands was identified in a letter from van Rensselaer to Johan de Laet (a partner in the Dutch West India Company) as *Pafraets Dael* (Pafraet's Part) in honor of van Rensselaer's mother, but the first Rensselaerswyck settlers on the east side of the river established themselves across from the fort. Settlers in Rensselaerswyck were generally there at the discretion of the patroon. They were lent livestock, a house and a barn but were required to pay rents and keep their homes, barns and fences in good repair and their fields planted. Rents might include money, labor, beaver, wampum or a portion of the farm's produce. Local mills, owned by the patroon but operated by others, held a monopoly on milling grains and sawing lumber.

Officials of the Dutch West India Company, who had built Fort Orange, also held a monopoly on the European side of the lucrative fur trade. Van Rensselaer uneasily accepted this arrangement and seems to have focused on his agricultural pursuits, even going so far as to expressly prohibit his colonists from engaging in the fur trade. It should be noted that nearly half of the immigrants to this area were not really Dutch but came from areas in France, Germany and the Spanish Netherlands that bordered the Netherlands. These Rensselaerswyck settlers routinely saw their Mohican neighbors profiting from the trade in which they were forbidden to participate. So in time, local Indian people, ex-company officials and farmers began trading at the periphery of Fort Orange, in violation of the company's monopoly. These early trader-farmers were joined by laborers and craftsmen: first sawyers, millers and laborers, and eventually blacksmiths, locksmiths, weavers, tailors, shoemakers and a brewer arrived.

One of these men was Lubbert Gijsbertz, who brought his wife and children to Rensselaerswyck to work as a wagon maker and wheelwright. He would give his name to Lubberde's landt, between the Poesten Kill and Wynants Kill. Another was the carpenter Thomas Chambers, who built the first farm on the Poesten Kill. The patroon also arranged for the continual purchase and transport to his colony of a variety of animals, horses, cows and all manner of goods necessary to operate the farms. Thousands of bricks, ironwork, weapons, lead, pots, tools, brewing and distilling equipment and supplies, blankets, clothing, cloth, seed, spices, cheese, soap, oils and grape and tobacco seedlings were sent in the 1630s. There were about one hundred people living in the entire colony in 1642; ten years later there were more than twice that number, and by 1660, although there are no numbers for the East Manor, Beverwijck (outside the walls of Fort Orange) was a large village of about one thousand people.

When land was considered for new farms in the East Manor, the land the Mohican were cultivating above the Poesten Kill to Uñuwat's Castle was out of the question. The land to the south between the Poesten Kill and Wynants Kill (near Dickops) was apparently not permanently inhabited, however, and it was here that the first farm on the east side of the Hudson north of present-day Rensselaer was located. The terms of the contract with the officers of Rensselaerswyck are found in the Van Rensselaer Bowier Manuscripts, dated September 7, 1646. The land was described as "situated obliquely opposite the farm called de Vlackte, on the east side of the river, between the two creeks." The contract provided that Thomas Chambers (an English carpenter) would be allowed

The Poesten Kill

This photograph of the Poesten Kill near the village of Poestenkill was taken during dredging in the twentieth century but probably resembles the way the lower Poesten Kill near the Hudson looked at low water in the 1600s. *Courtesy Poestenkill Historical Society.*

to use the farm for a period of five years beginning November 1, 1647. He was, however, required to build at his own expense a sixty- by twenty-eight-foot barn, a thirty-two- by eighteen-foot dwelling house, hay barracks and a fence. At the end of the five-year contract, Chambers was required to turn over this property to the patroon in lieu of rent, along with two mares, two stallions and four cows lent him by the patroon, and twenty-five pounds of butter—plus annual tithes.

There is no record of a formal purchase of the Chambers lands from the Mohican, and this may have strained relations with them. Chambers complained of being harassed and having animals killed by the Mohican in 1648 and 1649. The harassing parties may have had kinship ties to those living at Unuwat's Castle who were using the grounds at Chambers's doorstep for food and water. Between 1651 and 1708, most of what is now Troy was acquired by the Europeans from more than seventy-five individual Mohican from at least thirty families. Regardless of the cause of the conflict, the Mohican challenge to Thomas Chambers's farm had the desired effect, and in January 1651 the officers of the colony made the effort to purchase the Wynants Kill from the Indians.

It seems likely that the home Chambers built between the two kills was not in a Dutch style at all, but more probably English. It almost certainly still had the common steep-pitched roof but was probably sided with English-style clapboards. In the 1600s, area residents often had unique nicknames that made it easy to identify them in local records. Chambers was nicknamed *Clabbordt*, a corruption of the English term clapboard, and he is said to have introduced clapboard siding to the colony. Among the records left from the era is a 1642 agreement between Chambers and Jan Jansen Schepmoes to build Schepmoes's house in New Amsterdam (New York City) and cover it with five hundred clapboards.

Chambers stayed on the farm until the summer of 1654, when he surrendered the house, barn and hay barracks, signed a note to Jan Baptist van Rensselaer for the rent he still owed and made a fateful move to the Esopus River. In the fall of 1654, following the departure of Thomas Chambers, Jan Barentse Wemp contracted with the patroonship (Jan Baptist van Rensselaer and his brother Jeremias had by then succeeded their father) to lease the Chambers farm. The lease, which ended the first day of May 1661, included the house, barn, hay barracks and about sixty acres of "land between the two creeks as cultivated by Thomas Chambers." Wemp was an independent farmer-trader who arrived at Fort Orange about 1643 with money enough to pay his own passage (he leased his first farm from the patroon nearer Fort Orange). He was also known as Poest, a name that he may have given a gray mare in about 1651, and for which the Poesten Kill is named.

Wemp, and later his widowed wife Maritie, eventually had interests throughout the area that included houses in two local villages, farms, mills and several "farm servants," including Gerrit Gysbertsz (Gysbertsen) and Sweer Theunissen van Velson. During his tenure on the Poesten Kill, Wemp amassed enough local prestige to deal with the Mohican directly, under his own name, for lands to the north of his farm. In his contract with the colony, he was encouraged to negotiate with the Mohican for land above the Poesten Kill to add to his farm under the same terms "if adjoining land can be obtained from the savages." This he succeeded in doing, and in 1659 he purchased land "beginning from the mill on the [Poesten Kill] creek and to goe over the sd: Creek unto the great meadow ground whereabout sixty six paces the trees are marked." The land became known as the Poesten Bouwerie, and Wemp hired Cornelis Woutersz to make considerable repairs to the barn.

What these farms looked like is only conjecture at this point, as there has been virtually no archaeology aimed at the Dutch period along the Poesten Kill. Two similar farms in the East Manor have been found, but neither may reflect the kind of buildings that the English carpenter Thomas Chambers built on the Poesten Kill. Neither of the farms has been excavated, but new books by Shirley Dunn, James W. Bradley and the work of archaeologists Paul Huey and the firm Hartgen Archaeological Associates have painted a picture of what some of the Poesten Kill's farms probably looked like. "Most of the farms were modest size, fifty to sixty acres, and had a standard set of buildings invariably described as 'a house, barn, and hay barracks,'" according to James W. Bradley's *Before Albany*. "This suggests that the people and animals lived in separate buildings in contrast to a 'large farmhouse' (or *hallehuis*) where everyone lived together under one big roof."

Women's work was difficult on the Poesten Kill in the Dutch era. They ran the household and raised the children they generally had every other year. Cleaning, washing, ironing, sewing, knitting and food preparation took up much of their time, and women were experts at the complicated feat of keeping kitchen fires burning at various temperatures throughout the day. Cooking included daily meals, regular baking and processing foods for winter storage. Women often represented their husbands in public and business matters when necessary and served as partners in the family farm business. Janny Venema, in her recent history *Beverwijck: A Dutch Village on the American Frontier, 1652–1664*, noted that "marriage in the Dutch Republic, perhaps more so than in the rest of Europe, was based on partnership and mutual duties and responsibilities," something that carried over to Rensselaerswyck. Many women worked for wages or barter cleaning, doing laundry, producing textiles and as maids and wet nurses. In the 1650s, some women in Beverwijck ran taverns, were members of local guilds and participated in retail trades.

Women on the Poesten Kill planted and tended the gardens and may have also fed the livestock, collected eggs and aided in the slaughter of animals. Adriaen van der Donck mentioned the kinds of vegetables that were grown by the inhabitants of Rensselaerswyck in the 1650s: "various kinds of salads, cabbages, parsnips, beets, endive, succory, finckel, sorrel, dill, spinage, radishes, Spanish radishes, parsley, chervil (or sweet cicely), cresses, onions, leeks, and besides what is commonly found in kitchen garden." Herb gardens might include "rosemary, lavender, hyssop, thyme, sage, marjoram, balm, holy onions, wormwood, belury, chives, and clary; also pimpernel, dragon's blood, five-finger, tarragon, etc., together with laurel, artichokes, and asparagus, and various other things," including of course pumpkins, squash, cucumbers, corn, small fruits, apples, cherries and other fruit trees.

While farming was an important component of economic survival, one of Jan Wemp's primary goals in obtaining this spot on the Poesten Kill was to improve his access to the Indian trade. "He craftily sent out word to the Indians that he would pay the highest prices for their furs and that by dealing with him they would not only secure better bargains but be saved the trouble of traveling through to the fort," Troy historian George Baker Anderson wrote in 1897. "The traders of Fort Orange soon found that their rival… had found a location where he could intercept a large number of the Indians on their way to the original post, and they immediately began to make complaints to the agents of the patroon." Once established on the Poesten Kill, Wemp bargained with the Mohawk to the west of Fort Orange for lands at a better location to intercept the fur trade (at what is now Schenectady) and received part of the first patent for land there in 1662.

The demise of the fur trade in the late 1650s and the British takeover of Fort Orange in 1664 led to increased consolidation of economic activity in Beverwijck and provided impetus for more settlement in the East Manor. Those conditions were magnified by an animosity between the patroon and the Dutch West India

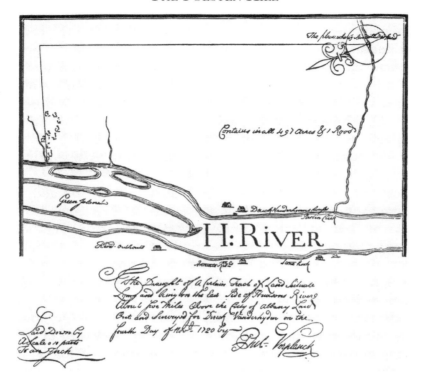

This 1720 survey of the nearly five-hundred-acre farm of Dirck van der Heyden was one of the first to show the then meandering mouth of the Poesten Kill, here labeled "Poesten Creek." *Courtesy Troy Public Library.*

Company that led to the latter allowing more land purchases from the Indians by private individuals outside Beverwijck. This policy probably encouraged Wemp to leave Rensselaerswyck to establish himself in Schenectady in 1662. Wemp was a relatively wealthy man when he died in 1663, no mean feat at a time when economic hardship was on the increase (cases of personal debt more than doubled at the Beverwijck court in 1658, the first full year of declining beaver trade). He owned a house and lot in Beverwijck, his farm on the Poesten Kill and the farm in Schenectady. He also owned a scow, a small sailing craft, which was sold to Jan Cornelissen van der Heyden and his brother Poulus Cornelissen. Wemp's farm on the Poesten Kill was increasingly the basis of land speculation in the decades to follow.

After Jan Barentse Wemp's death, his widow Maritie Myndertse remarried to Wemp's former farm hand, Sweer Theunissen van Velson. Before the marriage, they signed a prenuptial agreement, which stipulated that on the event of her death, he would not interfere with the inheritance of her children and would pay two hundred beavers to them from the sale of her possessions. It was also stipulated that "all other property which they may acquire together shall be enjoyed and divided by them both and their heirs." The idea of property during the early settlement of the Poesten Kill can be confusing. Originally, land was granted by the Dutch government to the Dutch West India Company (Fort Orange). In 1629, large manors were allowed to members of the company; van Rensselaer secured his from the Mohican beginning in 1630 to create Rensselaerswyck. In exchange for his new manor, van Rensselaer was required to settle fifty people. Chambers and Wemp *owned* the land only in the sense that they had the rights to it—these agreements would today be considered *leases*, although they were in many ways treated as *sales*. It makes for a somewhat confusing history of local land transfers. Following the takeover by the English in 1664, the patroonship system was allowed to continue (though there were only two actual patroons left by that time), and the British began giving large grants to influential colonials.

By the time of the English takeover, Sweer Theunissen van Velson was in a sense an absentee landlord of the Poesten Bowery, which then included both sides of the Poesten Kill south to the Wynants Kill; it ranged from near the Poesten Mill at the base of the plateau on the bowery's east side (today, Hill Street) to the Hudson River. Van Velson secured his leased rights by a patent from Richard Nicolls, the English governor of the province of New York. About the same time, van Velson leased the section to the south of the Poesten Kill, known then as Lubberde's landt, from Johanna de Laet Ebbingh, the daughter of Johan de Laet. In the late 1660s, however, van Velson gave up his lease of the south side of the Poesten Kill and began subleasing his lands on the north side. Two lots were initially occupied by his stepson, Jacob Heven. Wemp's old house and lot were leased for 250 beavers to Pieterse van Woggelum, another land speculator from Albany, in 1671. Van Woggelum owned rights to the mill on the Wynants Kill for a short time and secured the rest of the north side of the Poesten Kill from van Velson in 1679. Two years later, van Woggelum added the mostly forested land north of the Poesten Kill from Robert Saunders (with the approval of the English governor Sir Edmund Andros). Woggelum subleased his farm first to Andries Albertsz Bratt in 1682, and then to the tailor Joachim Ketelhuyn the following year and for six years thereafter.

Meanwhile, the south side of the Poesten Bowery had been conveyed by Jeronimus Ebbingh (husband of Johanna de Laet) to Jurian Teunisse Tappan, an innkeeper and speculator in real estate, in July 1676. Tappan had already been leasing the bowery, along with his house, barn, two hay ricks, eight draft horses and four cows. The next year, Tappan sold his rights in the farm, including the grain that had been already sowed, "and all that is thereon fast by earth and nailed," to trader and land speculator Philip Pieterse Schuyler.

In 1690, Sweer Theunissen van Velson was killed with his wife, Maritie Myndertse, and four African slaves in the Indian attack on Schenectady, as was Jan Wemp's son Myndert. Without heirs, the old Wemp farm on the Poesten Kill fell into the hands of Wemp's son-in-law, Captain Johannes Wendell, an alderman in Albany who administered the estate. Johannes Wendell had already purchased the lands from Woggelum's farm north to the present Waterford Bridge from Robert Sanders. He and his son Robert Wendell held these lands for more than eighty years and eventually sold the northern portion to Jacob Lansing in 1763.

THE VAN DER HEYDEN ESTATE

By 1700, the Poesten Kill bottomlands were divided into several parcels. On the north side of the kill stood the van Woggelum farm, with its lands extending "two miles into the woods," and the Poesten Mill (operated by Albert Andries Bratt in 1684). On the Poesten Kill's south bank stood the Schuyler farm. The community also included unnamed servants, craftsmen, tradesmen, farmers, millers and their families (and likely a few slaves and Native Americans). A road, now Hill Street, angled (as it still does, out of line with the rest of Troy's streets) from the Poesten Mill northwest toward the Hudson to what would become van der Heyden's ferry landing. In 1707, the van Woggelum bowery was conveyed to Dirck van der Heyden, who was then taking over the best lands along the Hudson (he bought Schuyler's farm in 1720). Before it took the name Troy, the community that stretched from the Poesten Kill north to the Piscawan Kill was known as Vanderheyden.

Dirck van der Heyden was a frontier trader who sometimes ventured far from Albany to conduct his business. The northern part of the Poesten Bowery (known as Vanderheyden) was handed down over eighty years to the great-grandsons of Dirck van der Heyden. According to local historian Cuyler Reynolds, the van der Heydens "had secured the finest property within a radius of miles, and after the war of the revolution closed, and emigrants from New England began to arrive, they found no land for sale. Settlements were made all around the farm, but for a long time the van der Heydens would not part with an acre. There seems to be no doubt that the settlement of Troy was greatly retarded by the obstinacy of Jacob van der Heyden, so that Lansingburgh gained a great advantage." As late as 1875, officials at Troy were negotiating with van der Heyden heirs for a piece of land on which to build a new city hall at the southwest corner of Third and State Streets.

The farm between the Poesten Kill and what is now Division Street was owned by Matthias, or Mattys, van der Heyden. His farmhouse was a two-story wood structure that stood near the intersection of Second and Division Streets. In 1752, Mattys built a brick building on the east side of River Road at the corner of Division Street (now a Russell Sage parking lot). The brick building was rented in 1786 to Captain Stephen Ashley, who operated it as an inn. It was torn down in 1886 to serve as the location of a steam engine company. Owing to the meandering and periodic flooding of the Poesten Kill, the lower farm of Mattys and the farms south of the kill were generally less productive than the two upper farms of Jacob D. van der Heyden (who was called "the Patroon" by his neighbors) and, above his, the farm of Jacob I. van der Heyden.

With the ownership of the Poesten Kill's best lands and water rights already staked out, new settlers were generally forced to rent from the van der Heydens or move inland (and into the Hoosac Valley) and lease directly from the van Rensselaers. Those willing to take their chances on farms on the shallow, rocky, wet soils in the harsher climate of the plateau learned quickly, if they had not already known, to diversify the way in which they earned their livings. The mostly New Englanders and immigrants from what is now Germany farmed small plots and, when possible, applied for water rights from the patroon. Settlers along the Poesten Kill followed it downstream through what is now Brunswick to cross the Hudson at van der Heyden's in order to access the markets at Albany. The area was still considered a frontier, with all its attendant conflict between Native Americans, New France and the English colonies.

Normally, Dutch settlers had little concern with native people nearby. They often let them stay in their homes, sometimes in large numbers, but conflict was never far from their minds. In 1659, during the Dutch war with Indians at the Esopus, those living at Beverwijck built a palisade to protect the village "against attacks by the Indians

The Van der Heyden Estate

The original van der Heyden house, home to Dirck van der Heyden, was located on the middle farm of Jacob D. van der Heyden at what would later be the corner of River and Ferry Streets. It served as the Vanderheyden Ferry office beginning in 1789 and was torn down in the 1880s. *Courtesy Troy Public Library.*

in these dangerous times, and to have this defense built as speedily as possible with the materials at hand." Abraham Pietersz Vosburgh, then part owner of the mill on the Wynants Kill, was killed in the First Esopus War and Thomas Chambers was a witness/instigator to the war. In all, the First Esopus War cost the lives of thirteen men, many of the community's livestock and the burning of several outlying buildings. Chambers went on to be a prominent citizen and is considered a founder of Kingston. Following the Second Esopus War (which broke out in 1663), Chambers built a large stone mansion about a mile north of the Kingston stockade called Foxhall.

Throughout the English colonial era, lumberers, carpenters, joiners, masons and other building trades, along with shipping, warehousing, redistribution and crafts and service providers, served a constant building and transportation boom in Albany. The hinterlands along the Poesten Kill and other East Manor streams, however, were generally restricted by frontier raids, and in 1714 all of Rensselaerswyck contained only about 600 people. The uneasy peace reached at the Treaty of Utrecht ended Queen Anne's War in 1713 and allowed for the hesitant continuation of frontier settlement, but by 1744 England and France were at war again. The conflict was known as the War of the Austrian Succession in Europe and King George's War (1744–48) in North America once it began with a force of 4,300 New Englanders taking Louisbourg on Cape Breton Island. In the fall of 1745, the French resumed their raids on the New England and New York settlements.

That year, John Schuyler's plantation up the Hudson River at what is now Schuylerville was attacked by French and Native Americans under Paul Marin. Fort Saratoga was destroyed and 103 men were taken prisoner and marched north to Montreal. Some escaped, but a dozen or so took refuge in the cellar of Schuyler's house and were killed when it was burned to the ground, including Schuyler himself. That same year, Hoosick was attacked and burned; the following year six members of the van Iveren family were killed near what is now Defreestville. Similar attacks from Schaghtticoke to Nassau caused a great panic and desertion among many of the settlers of their lands along the upper Poesten Kill and the plateau. It was at this time that John van Rensselaer fortified his house, now known as Fort Crailo, and it became a regular mustering place for local militia. Although territorial disputes continued over the boundary between New France and the British colonies, the Treaty of Aix-la-Chapelle effectively ended the raids in 1748.

The French and Indian War (1754–63) saw larger armies take the field and reduced considerably the number of raiding parties acting south of Fort Edward, but still the line of settlement had only barely begun to extend from the Hudson River onto the Rensselaer plateau above. The threat of direct conflict was still real, and in 1754, Indians raided Petersburg, killing and capturing many residents. The war's impact on local and regional in-migration perhaps had a greater effect, however. British and Irish soldiers serving in the war and former New England militiamen, along with people from New York City, Long Island and the middle colonies, including large numbers of people from what is now Germany, began arriving and passing through the area before the Revolution as refugees and opportunists.

NEW FARMS ON THE
UPPER POESTEN KILL

In 1750, there were about two thousand people in Albany, either as permanent residents or in the process of step migration. Its wharves were crowded with sloops, barges and scows, and lumberyards piled high with boards occupied the fields along the river. To supply this boom in the city and beyond, laboring, artisan, trade, merchant and professional occupations became more and more diverse before the Revolution. Making and repairing goods for the city's residents, the regional market and those passing through on their way to the frontier were primary occupations. Additionally, shipping, loading, unloading, warehousing and repacking for further shipment provided large numbers of jobs for pilots, crewmen, teamsters, craftspeople and laborers of all sorts.

The mouth of the Poesten Kill, on the other hand, had changed relatively little in the one hundred years that Europeans had been there. A scattering of farm buildings on the lower, middle and upper van der Heyden farms still stood north of the Poesten Kill. Among them was the ferry landing and the Hoosac Road running east, where the farm of Wilhalmus Smith stood, and north of him, Barnet Bratt. Some distance from the north bank of the Poesten Kill at Liberty Street was the home of Dirck van der Heyden (near Mount Ida) and Abraham van der Heyden.

The south side farm, initially centered on a house near the southwest corner of what are now First and Madison Streets, was then practically on the south bank of the Poesten Kill. It went through a series of transactions in the 1700s that demonstrate the era's real estate speculation. It was sold by Philip Pieterse Schuyler to Stephanis Groesbeck in 1711, and ten days later sold again to Myndert Schuyler and Peter van Brugh. Four years later, it was divided between them, van Brugh taking the northern part, later occupied by Teddy Maginnis. The rest of the farm remained in the extended Schuyler family, as it was sold to Henderick Oothout in 1730 and then to Edward Collins (grandson of Philip Pieterse Schuyler) in 1732. Collins sold out to Jan van Buren in 1748, and after van Buren died in 1795, his widow lived on the farm until the early 1800s. Meanwhile, in 1771, Stephen J. Schuyler purchased the northern part of the south farm from Sarah Maginnis, Teddy's widow, including the best watered lands to the east along the kill and against the hill. The old Schuyler family cemetery was located one block from the Poesten Kill at the corner of Madison and Fourth Streets into the mid-1800s.

More growth had occurred on the plateau above. A number of settlers had also already established themselves at Petersburgh, at the extreme northeast corner of the East Manor. A few scattered farms, mostly from the Dutch period, were located near what is now Defreestville. From the 1740s to the 1760s, a group of mostly Palatinate German immigrants began taking up farms at Haynersville in what is now the town of Brunswick, and the same thing was happening in all the communities along the Poesten Kill. East along the flats between Ida Lake and Eagle Mills, where the road to the Hoosac neared the Poesten Kill, stood the Watson farm. Where the Hoosac Road crossed the Poesten Kill tributary at Sweet Milk Creek was the home of David Benn. Five hundred acres on the "flatts" of the Poesten Kill at what was to become the area of Ida Lake was settled by John Fonda; the Fonda home stood near an early bridge crossing the Poesten Kill.

In the 1760s, it must have seemed that settlers were establishing farms everywhere. In 1763, Abraham Jacob Lansing purchased the Stone Arabia Patent (later New City, now Lansingburgh) north of Jacob van der Heyden's. In 1765, Stephen van Rensselaer began leasing the twelve-thousand-acre tract now known as Stephentown. All along the Poesten Kill and Wynants Kill, settlers began taking up patents from the patroon, a few applying for water rights. In

New Farms on the Upper Poesten Kill

Many of the millponds and raceways on the upper Poesten Kill served a variety of uses. This one on Plank Road east of Poestenkill Village was both a saw- and gristmill. *Courtesy Poestenkill Historical Society.*

1768, Joshua Lockwood and William Carpenter built the first gristmill at what is now West Sand Lake, perhaps the first mill in the region above the Hudson tidal flats. In 1767, the East Manor was surveyed by John R. Bleeker, and his resulting map included the names of some 130 families on the east side of the Hudson. The surge in growth before the Revolution led to the surveying of New City into 288 building lots in 1771 and its rapid growth into the area's largest village.

One of the craftsmen living temporarily in Albany before the American Revolution was the carpenter Archelaus Lynd. Lynd had come from England or Ireland to the city's lumbering district about 1750. After giving birth to a son, Aaron, in 1758, Archelaus's first wife died and he married again, this time to Mary Dovebach (Duivebach, Davenback). Following the marriage, the family left Albany and was leased 452 acres at the eastern edge of the plateau

along the north side of the Poesten Kill for two years. The Lynds
built a house near the naturally occurring sulfur spring and began
working a nearby piece of land at the foot of the hills from which
the Poesten Kill descended. The parcel, like those shown around
it on the John van Alen map of 1788, was a large, irregular plot.
The Poesten Kill made a natural boundary to the south and a line
of hills separated the Lynd parcel from that of Lazarus Ives, his
Connecticut neighbor to the north. To the west of Lynd was the
farm of David Berringer, who had come up from Kinderhook
and taken up 368 acres straddling the Poesten Kill. To the east
of the Berringers, across the kill from the Lynd parcel, were the

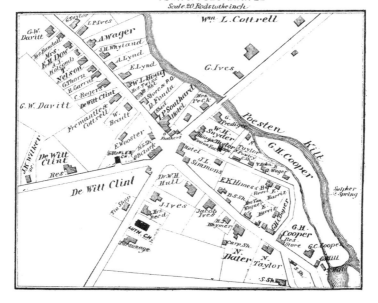

The village of Poestenkill is shown on this map from 1876 crowded along the
Poesten Kill. Note the sulfur spring and Cooper's millpond and the raceway, which
powered the village's water wheels. The house marked G. Ives is located where
Archelaus Lynd established an early farm. *Courtesy Poestenkill Historical Society.*

New Farms on the Upper Poesten Kill

lands of Henry Strunk and Garrett and Abraham Peek. Henry Strunk and his sister Catherine came from what is now northern Germany to New York City about 1750. Both served as indentured servants—Henry for five years, Catherine for three—in order to pay their way. In 1756, Henry married Anna Elizabeth Harwich in Albany and the two settled on an oddly shaped 269 acres he and his brother were granted to the south of the Lynd farm. The parcel's shape allowed them access to the kill near the center of what would become the hamlet of Poestenkill. The Peeks were to the east, with land also adjoining the kill.

By the time John van Alen finished his survey of Rensselaerswyck in 1788, the area that was to be the hamlet of Poestenkill was already settled by these five families. What's more, the map van Alen drew shows that a large number of family transfers of land had already taken place. Thirteen of the twenty-five parcels that lie entirely within the current Poestenkill town boundaries shared six surnames: Ives, Peek, Berringer, Muller, Jacobs and Cooper. In 1788, half of those living around what was to be the hamlet of Poestenkill lived next door to a relative. That was not the only defining social characteristic, though, because these families all raised large numbers of children. The Lynds, who lived the closest to the center of what would become the hamlet, had at least six children who lived into adulthood and possibly seven more from Archelaus's earlier marriage; a mile north, the Ives had at least five; just less than a mile east, the Berringers also had at least five; the Strunks a mile south had seven. Within about a two-mile radius in 1788, there were more than twenty-five to thirty children and over a dozen adults in the five families on whose land the hamlet of Poestenkill grew.

TROY

Another Village on the Poesten Kill

As the path toward the Revolution grew shorter, lines were drawn between settlers and raids became a fairly common occurrence in the early years of the war. In 1884, Catherine Schermerhorn Shipherd shared the following story in a letter to her granddaughter about the Fonda homestead on the Poesten Kill at the time of the Revolution:

> *The house was located on a flat of meadow, bordering on the north side of the Poestenkill, and the south bank of the Poestenkill Creek was a range of abrupt rocks, where the Tories concealed themselves, watching and waiting until the family should leave the house, so they could rush down and rob the premises. There were two brothers and the father at home, and being the Sabbath day, they went out at early eventide to make some calls, and the father, to bring up the cows, leaving the women alone. The robbers seized this opportunity and went into the house, setting a guard at each door while the rest ransacked from dome to base, taking whatever they wanted. My grandfather* [Derick I. van der Heyden] *unexpectedly arrived to call on his prospective bride* [Rachel Fonda]. *One of the men took the reins of the horse from his hands, bidding him go direct into the house, which he did, being only one against a party of seven thieves. After they had selected what they wanted, they went to the mother and two daughters and took all the jewelry on their persons, except from the daughter who later became my grandmother. As one of them*

Troy

took her hands to remove her rings, he looked into her face and said: "You are such a pretty girl, you may keep your rings."

According to family historians, Peter Fonda, then a somewhat feeble old man, shouted, "Must we give up without a fight?" The story continues,

The Tories took all the silver, linen and guns, and the silver knee buckles belonging to the old gentleman. The guns were afterward found hidden under the old wooden bridge, crossing the Poestenkill, where a more modern bridge now stands. The linen was discovered on the high bank on the opposite side of the creek. Later some of the thieves were caught, tried and sentenced to be hung. One of them returned to John Fonda one of the stolen knee buckles and a spoon, which are now in the possession of one of his descendants.

The raid on the Fonda farm was not the norm, however, and those along the Poesten Kill suffered few of the depredations of war on the homefront experienced by those in other parts of New York. Instead, they profited by supplying the northern army, of which Philip Schuyler (son of Albany's first mayor) was appointed quartermaster. In 1777, the northern army was encamped at Van Schaick's Island in the Hudson and local people were called on to supply milk, fruits, vegetables, meats and other goods. New York City was then in the hands of the British, and Burgoyne had advanced down the Champlain Valley and taken Fort Edward. His force of some six to eight thousand men seemed poised to raid the Rensselaerswyck settlements, take Albany and cut the colonies in two along the Hudson River. It was at the Battles of Hubbarton and Bennington in Vermont and the final Battle of Saratoga that the manor was saved from the most serious ravages of the war. Many of the settlers along the Poesten Kill participated in these engagements.

The most significant changes brought by the American Revolution were demographic, as New England and middle colonies' soldiers provided a flood of new settlers moving into the region. Because the original Dutch settlers and those from before the Revolution had already taken up the best lands, many of these new settlers were forced to take up more marginal lands along the upper Poesten Kill and Wynants Kill drainage basins. The population exploded after the American Revolution. There had been about 600 people in all of Rensselaerswyck (both sides of the Hudson River) in 1714; in 1767, about 130 families lived in the East Manor.

In 1787, surveyor Flores Bancker laid out a village in the style of Philadelphia, with "regular squares and rectangular streets," on Jacob D. van der Heyden's middle farm. Over the next few years, more settlers arrived to build homes, stores, small businesses and warehouses. In 1789, at a meeting at Ashley's Tavern, the community was renamed Troy. By 1795, local papers included advertisements for a baker, dry goods and grocery merchants, a hatter and makers of saddles, harnesses and "sealskin, leather and oil cloth trunks." A visitor noted that already "tan-yards, potash works, rope walks, and mills are either in full work or building." To this list we should add a brickworks (at the foot of Ida Hill), cooperages, blacksmiths, shoe and shirt makers and at least a few slaughterhouses established before the war. There was also an assortment of taverns, inns, churches, civic societies and buildings, a central market, banks, bakeries and various milliners, merchants, shopkeepers and printers, all north of the Poesten Kill. Troy was experiencing unprecedented growth, and in 1797 the village's first resident newspaper, the *Farmer's Oracle*, reported on the flood of emigrants arriving at the Troy docks: "During the last forty-eight hours there have upwards of forty vessels arrived at this port," the paper reported, "the most of which are from New England States, with families on their way to settle our northern frontiers."

With the influx of settlers, speculators, boatmen, merchants, mechanics and laborers of all sorts came entrepreneurs ready to exploit the local water power on both the Poesten and Wynants Kills. In 1789, David De Freest built a fulling mill on the Wynants Kill, and in 1796 Thomas L. Whitbeck established a flouring mill there and David Buel the area's second paper mill. In 1799, the first dam was built on what would later be known as Glass Lake (the Rensselaer Glass Works was established in 1806), and in 1807 the first iron mill on the Wynants Kill began operating (later the Albany Rolling and Slitting Mill). In 1809, the Troy Iron and Nail Factory (later known as the Burden Iron Company) opened on the south side of Wynants Kill's upper falls.

TRANSPORTATION

The Engine of Commerce

Development along the Poesten Kill and of Rensselaer County more generally was boosted by its location at the head of transportation routes to the rest of the state, even before the construction of the Erie and Champlain Canals. A significant part of the commerce at the lower Poesten Kill was centered on the Hudson River. Jan Wemp had owned a small sailing scow in the late 1600s. His successor on the Poesten Kill, van Woggelum, was described in early records as a boatman and, in 1684, master of the open boat *Uhtty* plying between Albany and New York. A significant business in the area was the Vanderheyden Ferry, which provided the impetus for economic development all along the Poesten Kill and throughout Rensselaerswyck. A string of commercial buildings emerged near the ferry landing and along the start of the road to the Hoosac River. In 1786, Benjamin Thurber, a New Englander, built a small building and began advertising his "New Cash Store…at the sign of the Bunch of Grapes, at the Fork of Hoosick Road, near Jacob [I.] Vanderheyden's with East, West India, and European Goods of all kinds. For which he will receive, in lieu of Cash, black salts, Shipping Furs, Wheat, Corn, Rye, Butter, Cheese, Tallow, Hog's lard, Gammons, Pork, Bees-Wax, and old Pewter. He also continues to receive ashes, as usual, to supply his new erected Pot and Pearl Ash factory" at the mouth of the Hoosac.

The growth of New City (Lansingburgh) increased pressure on the van der Heydens to sell lots near the ferry landing, and in the late 1780s, the van der Heydens began dividing their land. Captain

Transportation

Stephen Ashley took over management of the Vanderheyden Ferry and kept a tavern. In 1788, Matthias van der Heyden reported that his boat "will ever be in readiness directly opposite the house at present occupied by...Ashley. The terms of crossing will be as moderate as can reasonably be expected, and a considerable allowance made to those who contract for the season." A secondary news note indicated that "notice for crossing will be given by sounding a conch-shell a few minutes before the boat starts." The Vanderheyden Ferry was by then carrying a considerable carting and pedestrian traffic, along with wagons and horses, between Albany and the East Manor, New City and the Hossac Valley.

In 1798, Mahlon Taylor, who was responsible for much of the development of the Poesten Kill in the early 1800s, established a competing ferry at the foot of Washington Street, which became known locally as the South Ferry. It was operated by Asahel House in 1800 and later was served by a small steam ferry for passengers. Another ferry was on the south side of the Poesten Kill, and its wharf was utilized by the mills along the Poesten Kill for their shipping needs, including the Clinton Stove Works, beside which it stood. Additional ferries came and went, and in 1854 the van der Heydens had their ferry monopoly stripped from them in the Supreme Court. By the late 1880s, there were four ferries running at Troy, including the one at the mouth of the Poesten Kill.

Although Lansingburgh was still the larger community, until the construction of the State Sloop Lock at the Piscawen Kill it could not handle larger vessels, and during the first part of the 1800s its dockside was considerably silted in to the point that jetties had to be built. Troy, on the other hand, was emerging as a substantial shipping port and was doing a brisk business in warehousing and transporting goods to and from ports as distant as New York City and New England. In 1790, Lansingburgh became the first incorporated village in the state of New York and in 1791, Rensselaer County was established. By 1800, there were perhaps 1,500 people in the village of Troy alone. By 1820, there were more than 5,200 and more than twice that number by 1830, when some eighty sloops were operating between Troy and New York City. By 1840, the population was almost four times as large as immigrants

This bridge spanned the Poesten Kill at Pawling Avenue. A dam below the bridge was constructed to supply a power tunnel built by Benjamin Marshall in 1840. *Courtesy Troy Public Library.*

flooded in from Ireland, Scotland, England and Northern Europe. Troy was the fourth wealthiest city per capita in the United States and an important port and increasingly important location for milling and manufacturing.

Captain Benjamin Allen commanded one of the earliest commercial shipping vessels, the sixty-ton schooner *Flora*, which he kept anchored near the ferry. The *Flora* carried out mostly grain (though often other local goods) and returned with foreign and domestic manufactured products. The shopkeeper Benjamin Covell, for instance, engaged Allen to bring beaver and raccoon skins to his brother Silas in Providence and to return with tanned sheepskins, leather gloves, writing paper and spelling books. In 1787, Yalles Mandeville and Casper Frats established a schooner line to transport freight and passengers between the ferry landing and New York. The sloop *Joanna* carried freight and passengers soon after, and by 1795, a single edition of the *Troy Recorder* was reporting the return of several Troy sloops: *Success* (Captain Benjamin), *Commerce* (Captain McCoun), *Emila* (Captain Wilson),

Transportation

Sally (Captain Baker), and a fifth unnamed vessel operated by Captain Hudson. By 1800, a shipyard existed north of the ferry near the corner of Fulton and Front Streets, where many sloops were built to carry lumber, grain, furs and potash from the surrounding countryside. Storehouses were built nearby and the Hudson River shoreline was piled high with lumber ready to ship, mostly sawn along the Poesten Kill.

In 1812, just five years after Robert Fulton and Robert Livingston's *North River Steamboat of Cleremont* made the first successful steamboat trip from New York to Albany, their steam-powered *Fire-Fly* began making regular trips between Troy and Albany. The twenty-year monopoly on steam transportation first granted to Robert Livingston and Robert Fulton was declared unconstitutional in 1824 by chief justice of the Supreme Court John Marshall, and almost immediately the Troy Steamboat Company was organized. By the end of the year, the *Chief Justice Marshall* had been acquired from a New York shipyard. It arrived at the Ferry Street wharf in the spring of 1825 after burning forty cords of pine wood on the sixteen-hour trip upriver. In the summer of 1826, the first steam ferry began operating, and the following year, the steamboat *Star* was built at the Troy shipyard by William Annesley to make trips between Troy and Albany. By 1844, Troy was home to eight passenger steamboats, ten towing steamboats, twenty-four freight barges and as many as one hundred sailing sloops, schooners and other large vessels. Many of them plied the recently built pier and boat basin at the mouth of the Poesten Kill.

As with today, the primary roads into the countryside left Troy north along River Street, east from Hoosick Street and from the top of Congress Street on Ida Hill. Beginning in the 1790s, a number of turnpikes were chartered by the state legislature to improve the flow of traffic between the growing communities in the upper Hudson Valley. The Albany and Schenectady Turnpike (today's Route 5), Great Western Turnpike (Route 20 West), Columbia Turnpike (Route 20 East), Eastern Turnpike (Bath, Sand Lake, Nassau, Berlin), Northern Turnpike (Lansingburgh, Routes 40, 67 and 22, Salem, Vermont), Stephentown Turnpike and the Troy and Schenectady Turnpike were all chartered between 1795 and 1802.

The bridge crossing the Poesten Kill at the flats (today the Pawling Avenue Bridge) was a significant thoroughfare, even before the Sand Lake Turnpike was formally established in 1822, as a bridge at or near there had stood since before the American Revolution. In the 1860s and until it was replaced by a stone bridge in the late 1880s, this bridge was known as the "Red Bridge." The improved turnpike left the bridge and ran to Wynants Kill and on to what is now West Sand Lake, where it connected with the Eastern Turnpike running from the Hudson Ferry at Bath to Berlin. Additional turnpikes were authorized to connect Troy with the areas along the upper Poesten Kill with good roads. In 1831, the Troy Turnpike went from Troy to Bennington, Vermont (along what is today generally Route 7). The Brunswick and Pittstown Turnpike was incorporated to build a road from Eagle Mills to the road to Hoosick in Pittstown. Two other early roads went to Eagle Mills from the Poesten Kill at Ida Hill: Pinewoods Avenue (probably older) and the current Route 2, part of the Brunswick and Pittstown Turnpike. The Troy and Berlin Turnpike was chartered in 1833 along Spring Avenue to connect the Pawling Avenue bridge with Poestenkill Village and then over the mountains along Plank Road to Berlin. In 1835, the Petersburg, Grafton and Brunswick Turnpike was chartered to connect the Brunswick and Pittstown Turnpike with Petersburg and Grafton.

The earliest bridge crossing the Poesten Kill almost certainly stood near the old Poesten Mill; it was a covered bridge in 1838. An early rough bridge probably crossed the lower Poesten Kill at River Street by the early 1700s. A bridge crossing the Poesten Kill near the bottom of the High Falls was built in the early part of the 1800s and allowed workers living on the Poesten Kill's south side direct access to the mills opposite throughout the century. Later, bridges would be built across the Poesten Kill at First, Second, Third and Fourth Streets, but as late as 1845, only River and Fourth Streets were bridged. The bridge at Second Street was built by 1869, and the one at Third probably in the early 1870s. The Fourth Street

Transportation

The low water and the friendly dog beneath this bridge on Farm-to-Market Road in Poestenkill Village are deceptive. William McChesney lost his life on a bridge here during the flood of 1891 when it was washed away beneath his feet. *Courtesy Poestenkill Historical Society.*

Bridge was also known as the "Red Bridge" in the late nineteenth and early twentieth centuries. In 1884, brothers Martin and Thomas Hersey were shot to death on the Red Bridge by a twenty-one-year-old German immigrant, Julius Siebolt.

Wooden bridges throughout the towns of Brunswick and Poestenkill were probably constructed during the 1760s as settlers flooded into what would become those towns. A covered bridge was once located at the tollgate before Eagle Mills on the Pittstown Turnpike (now Route 2 near Shippey Lane) where the turnpike crossed the Poesten Kill. The covered bridge was swept away in the flood of 1891 and was later replaced by a bridge painted white, giving this location the name "White Bridge." The tollgate keeper's home still stands nearby. Along the upper Poesten Kill, particularly at the villages of Eagle Mills and Poestenkill, the bridges were crucial links for commerce. Colliers, loggers, lumberers and farmers all depended on the bridges to get their products to market. New bridges were costly and bridge replacement time meant much

A temporary bridge was constructed during the replacement of the bridge in Poestenkill Village in the twentieth century. *Courtesy Poestenkill Historical Society.*

discussion and debate. In 1940, when the old iron bridge at Eagle Mills was in need of replacement, bonds were issued for $6,000, but the actual cost came in at $8,000. During construction, a temporary pontoon bridge was built upstream.

Another significant transportation development was the opening of the Erie and Champlain Canals to area traffic in 1823 (a canal between Troy and Boston had been proposed in 1819 but never materialized). The Erie Canal in particular was important because the falls at Cohoes inhibited travel west except by road. The canal was such a success that the state began enlarging it in 1836, but by the time it finished in 1862 the railroads were already taking over much of the canal business; the trip from New York to Buffalo was cut from ten days by canal to eleven hours by rail. The railroad era began in the area with the Rensselaer and Saratoga (R&S), which was completed in 1835. Initially the R&S ran from the eastern end of the new Troy and Green Island Bridge to Ballston Spa, where passengers disembarked for coaches to Saratoga. The R&S was joined in 1836 by the Troy & Schenectady Railroad, which carried more than half a million passengers and over 300,000 tons of freight in 1862. Ten years later, it was leased to the Delaware and Hudson Railroad (D&H), which operates it to this day.

Another line whose rail bed is still in use (by Conrail) is the Troy & Greenbush Railroad (T&G). The T&G arose from the incorporation of the New York & Albany Railroad in 1832, which was allowed to build a line from the Harlem River to Troy. The portion below Greenbush was delayed for a number of years but the rails between there and Troy were laid in 1840–41. The line extended from the Albany & West Stockbridge Railroad in Greenbush along River Street to its depot on King Street at the Green Island Bridge. A block south of the Poesten Kill, at the corner of Madison and River Streets, the T&G divided and crossed the kill in two places, at River and First Streets. The current First Street Bridge is made of square cut limestone (and an enlarged concrete section). It is believed to have been built in 1845 and still stands, although the tracks now end where they once crossed the kill at an angle. As late as the 1880s, the First Street Bridge was only used for rail traffic.

The T&G's bread and butter was initially passenger traffic. In the first six months of operation, the railroad's three engines and two "Troy-built cars, handsomely furnished and commodious," traveled nearly fourteen thousand miles carrying passengers, but just five hundred carrying freight. Two blocks north of the Poesten Kill, between Jefferson and Adams Streets along both sides of River Street, the T&G built a freight house, depot, machine shop, engine and car shops, a turntable, several wood sheds and a large rail yard—the entire complex was destroyed by fire in 1854. The line, however, was by then already leased to the Hudson River Railroad, with only the business between Troy and Albany being retained by the T&G. The line's trains were drawn by horses from the Poesten Kill depot north up River Street.

The depot on Adams Street was a significant station for South Troy. For example, when John A. Griswold died in 1872, his body was carried from the funeral at the Fifth Street Presbyterian Church on a bier to the Adams Street station. About three thousand ironworkers, managers, trustees and directors of the various companies he was associated with formed an escort that preceded the coffin to the station. There it was loaded on a car hung for mourning, and the attached cars were loaded with friends and family to take Griswold's body to Oakwood Cemetery. Eventually the area east of the depot along the Hudson was filled, and the rail yards were expanded to take up the entire area between River Street and the river from below Jefferson Street to Adams, making the T&G complex one of the largest on the lower Poesten Kill. The railroad's freight operations also spilled over to the alley between River and First Streets (between Ida and Adams Streets) to such an extent that the city was forced to pass a law forbidding the alley's use by the company.

In 1860, the City of Troy authorized the Troy & Lansingburgh Railroad Company (T&L, later part of the Union Traction Company) to build horse-powered streetcar lines from Lansingburgh along Twentieth and River Streets to and along Adams Street to Second Street and from there south to the Wynants Kill. In 1866, the Troy and Albia Horse Railroad Company was allowed to lay track from the tracks of the T&L on River Street up Congress Street to the Pawling Avenue Bridge. The following year, another line was authorized in North Troy to connect with Congress Street, and in 1890 the Albia line was extended north to Ferry Street and also to Hoosick Street north from Ida Hill. It was at this time that the most of the homes in the Pawling Avenue neighborhood were built. So began the extension of the streetcars throughout the area, reaching as far into the countryside as Averill Park, north to and along Hoosick Street and on to Waterford and south to the Wynants Kill.

In 1887, the Troy and Albia line was operating eleven cars with some fifty horses on just three miles of track from River Street to Pawling Avenue. These lines were all run by horse until the completion of electrical power systems in the 1890s, and in 1895

Transportation

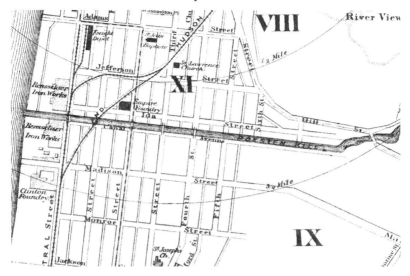

This 1880 map of the neighborhood at the lower Poesten Kill shows the foundries, the Troy & Greenbush Railroad and depot and the trolley line running along Adams Street and down Second. The missing alleyway between Third and Fourth Streets was the location of an early millpond. *Courtesy Troy Public Library.*

the Troy & New England Railway Company began operating an electric trolley line between Troy and Averill Park along the Albia line. These lines, along with nearly all the local trolley lines between Albany and Lake George, were consolidated under the United Traction Company in 1899. Despite numerous labor struggles and strikes, the line to Averill Park ran until 1925, when bus service was begun between Glass Lake and Troy. In 1932, the trolley service ended in Troy (the last cars ran in Albany in 1946), and with the closing of Troy's Union Station in 1955, the age of passenger service to the lower Poesten Kill had come to an end.

EARLY POESTEN
KILL MILLS

Most of the commercial and residential development along the Poesten Kill after the American Revolution took place near the ferry landing at Troy, principally along the Hudson River. Increasingly, warehouses and small shops lined the Hudson along River Street from Broadway south to Division. Here the shipping, carting and teaming of goods to an expanding America took place. South of Division Street along the Hudson, lumber dealers and their associated business congregated into a large lumber district. Piles of boards stood waiting to be shipped, and lumber sheds and offices were built, especially toward the Poesten Kill below Liberty Street on the blocks between River and Front Streets. Industrial development (mostly grist- and sawmills and later paper, textiles, iron and steel mills) centered on the Poesten Kill where dams and raceways were built. A separate shipping area with its own pier was established before 1800.

In the early 1600s, the patroon had hoped to install all of his experienced craftsmen across from Fort Orange. His first saw- and gristmills, built there in the early 1630s, were expected to produce enough merchantable lumber and flour to sell to the Dutch West India Company, the local Indians and the English. He hoped that local Indians would also bring their corn to be ground in exchange for wampum and lumber would be available to keep the colony growing. The patroon expanded his milling investments on the east side of the Hudson by encouraging the Poesten Kill's first European settler, Thomas Chambers, to build a sawmill on the

Early Poesten Kill Mills

Poesten Bowery. The Poesten Mill was located fifty-eight chains east of the Hudson (later Hill Street) and for the better part of two centuries was mentioned as a starting point for surveys of the land around the lower Poesten Kill.

After Jan Wemp, the Poesten Mill was operated by Sweer van Velson until he left for Schenectady, where he built that community's first gristmill. In 1675, van Velson sold his rights in the Poesten Mill to Jan Cornelise Vyselaer (also called Jan Gow or Gouw) and Lucas Pietersen Coeymans. The mill lands were described as "the sawmill together with the kill on which the mill stands and two morgens of arable land…together with free egress and a road along the hill, by Pieter Pieterse van Woggelum's, to the shore." Lucas Pietersen almost immediately conveyed his half stake in the mill to Andries Albertsen Bratt. In 1680, Jan Cornelise Vyselaer also conveyed his half of the mill to Bratt, including half of the Poesten Kill, half of the road and "half interest in the tools which belong to the aforesaid mill…with ten new saws…together with what has been added, built and delivered to the mill since [1675]…saving the lord's right." Four years later, Bratt attempted to purchase land described as "a piece of woodland…between the kill on which Andries Albertse Bratt's mill stood and the Piscawen Kill, extending from the claim or land of Peter van Woggelum, and two miles into the woods" from two Mohican men named Annape (or Alnape) and Amahamett. The land would have included Ida Hill and the Poesten Kill's flatlands to the east on the plateau, but the deed was apparently never executed. That same year Bratt sold half of the Poesten Mill (including its eleven saws, tools and half of the kill itself and the right of way) to Johannes Wendell.

The notice of the public sale of the sawmills in Greenbush in 1658 and an inventory of tools of Wynant Gerritsen van der Poel and Abraham Pietersen Vosburgh (owners of the sawmill on the Wynants Kill) indicate what kinds of tools were needed in these early mills: an iron crank (and sometimes an iron pinion), an iron rack or frame, about fifteen to twenty clamps (upper and lower), a wooden wheel, marking irons, about ten saws and wedges (including a handsaw and a crosscut saw), perhaps a dozen or more iron bars, one or two peaveys, cant hooks, sledgehammers, axes, a saw set and a small number of files for sharpening. Lumber sledges, wagons or sleighs and workhorses were also required, and with these implements the Poesten Mill was capable of sawing a fairly small number of boards, as is attested to by the conditions of the sale of a one-quarter interest in the sawmill on the Wynants Kill in 1688. The contract of that sale provided for delivery to the seller five hundred one-inch boards within six months and another three hundred boards a year after that. It seems likely that the mill on the Poesten Kill was capable of sawing perhaps four to five thousand boards a year.

The growth of Troy meant that the mills on the Poesten Kill were taxed to their limit in the decades before 1800. According to Troy historian A.J. Weise, Mahlon Taylor floated logs on the Poesten Kill to supply his sawmill. Most logs, however, were probably hauled by teams to the mills, where a rack or frame held them against a single upright saw powered by an overshot wheel. Eventually additional saws were added to form gang saws, which could saw a merchantable amount of lumber. It was at about this time that larger amounts of lumber from the Poesten Kill were likely transported to other parts of Rensselaerswyck and possibly to Albany and New York as well. While commercial production of lumber had been one of the smaller uses of the forest in the seventeenth and eighteenth centuries, during most of the 1800s lumber was piled high along the Hudson awaiting transport.

By the 1850s, perhaps a dozen lumber companies had congregated in the lumber district along the river between Division Street and the Troy & Greenbush Railroad yards. Behind these vast lumberyards stood smaller shops, grocers, three carpenters, a chair factory and a bell foundry. Sprinkled between these along River Street were an assortment of mostly wood and a few brick homes; along First Street and toward the east stood more substantial homes of mostly brick. In the alley between First and River Streets there were several tenements. The largest of these apartment buildings, owned by John M. Peck and located between Adams and Jefferson Streets, was made of brick and was home to ten families. Dozens of families lived in crowded conditions on the north side of the Poesten Kill in the lumber district. Considerably fewer buildings, about which almost nothing is known, were located on the Poesten Kill's south side.

Much of this area north of the Poesten Kill along the Hudson was destroyed in 1854 when a large fire broke out near the river on the corner of Front and Division Streets. It began in the brick steam planing mill of George Quiggin. The alarm was given, and as strong winds blew the flames east along the south side of Division Street to River Street, the fire was with great difficulty kept from crossing River Street. Instead, it continued south along the west side of River Street and engulfed the lumberyards lining the Hudson between Division and Liberty and consuming an estimated twenty million board feet of lumber. It crossed Liberty Street, destroyed the home of Moses I. Winne and then began to spread east to the alley between Second and Third Streets, destroying some two hundred buildings over sixteen blocks, including Edgerton, Sheldon & Osborn's (later Birge's) chair factory, the Troy & Greenbush Railroad's freight depot and machine shop, the new bell foundry of Jones & Hitchcock, Parmenter's machine shop and other valuable homes and businesses. The Park Presbyterian Church on Second Street near Adams, which had been consecrated only the day before, was barely saved by firemen and parishioners whose own homes were being destroyed. Fire companies came from Albany, West Troy, Cohoes, Lansingburgh and Waterford, and the fire was finally stopped a block north of the Poesten Kill at Jefferson Street—the north–south halfway point on the pier at the mouth of the Poesten Kill.

"IMPROVING" THE
LOWER POESTEN KILL

The period between 1790 and the 1830s saw the emergence of larger mills and manufactories on the lower Poesten Kill. These followed the improvement of shipping and warehousing infrastructure (docks, roads, bridges and railroads) and required that improvements to the waterworks (raceways, millponds and local canals) be made. Of the new settlers at Troy it was Mahlon Taylor, who arrived in the 1780s from New Jersey, who proved to be one of the most important to the industrial development of the lower Poesten Kill. Taylor recognized that the Poesten Kill's location would provide not only plenty of water power, but also space for shipping at the kill's mouth to send his goods to growing local and regional markets. In 1785, Taylor purchased eight acres of land from Matthias van der Heyden along the Hudson from the kill to what is now Washington Street. Then in 1792, he also purchased the old grist- and sawmill site on the Poesten Kill and rebuilt the neglected dam, channeling the water north into a new millrace parallel to the kill. He built new grist- and sawmills on this raceway, which he extended all the way to the Hudson River. In the spring of 1793, Taylor built what is thought to be the first paper mill on the race, the first in northern New York.

After its construction, Taylor's paper mill was almost immediately sold to four men: Albany printers George and Charles Webster (owners of the *Albany Gazette*) and Hartford Connecticut paper makers Perely Ensign and Ashbel Seymour. Paper for printing, wrapping goods and writing was in increasing demand, but

"Improving" the Lower Poesten Kill

acquiring the necessary rags was a difficult proposition and wood pulp had not yet come into use. To supply the paper mill, the owners took out ads in the local papers asking those in the surrounding area (particularly women, who were invited to see the mill) to save their rags and bits of cloth for purchase by the company. Brought to the mill, the owners promised three pence a pound for white, blue, brown and checked cloth. The shortage of rags was so acute in the emerging paper industry generally that before 1790, advertisements were placed in Albany for rags for a paper mill in Vermont. Troy postmaster David Buel, later owner of his own paper mill on the Wynants Kill, supported the local paper company by encouraging the collection of rags at his post office in 1801.

In the Webster, Ensign and Seymour mill, rags were beaten into a pulp in large vats of water from the Poesten Kill. It was then ladled into molds and the thin sheets interleaved with felt cloth and squeezed with heavy pressure to expel the water and further flatten the sheets, which were then hung to dry. The paper mill on the Poesten Kill could make about five to ten reams a day, six days a week, mostly for Webster's *Albany Gazette*. The mill probably employed a dozen or more men and boys with two vats and wages were considered relatively high. Several paper mills were also built over the years on the Wynants Kill, including those of David Buel (about 1810) and Alexander and William Orr (1837), who claimed the first cylinder printing of wall paper and to be the first to add wood pulp to the paper process. Before 1855, a paper mill was also built on the Quacken Kill, east of Cropseyville.

Initially, improvement of the water power on the Poesten Kill was engineered and constructed by individual mill owners. Those at the base of the gorge were probably similar to one built by Thomas Whitbeck for his flouring mill on the Wynants Kill in 1796, described as a "trunk made of juice boards and plank." After this was washed away in the flooding of 1814, Elisha Putnam built in its place a conduit made of headless barrels placed end to end. Later the millrace seems to have dug into the ground, and in the late 1820s local mill owners began organizing themselves to accomplish the improvement of local water power. In 1826, Oliver Boutwell organized the Troy Hydraulic Company, perhaps to regulate the water of the Poesten Kill (the same year the Lansingburgh Dry Dock and Hydraulic Company and the Cohoes Company were incorporated). Later, Oliver Boutwell joined the Lansingburgh organization and the name was changed to the Troy Hydraulic Company in 1832, when it was granted control of half the Hudson's surplus water for 999 years by the New York State Canal Board. In 1829, the Wynants Kill Association was formed by twenty-three parties with a purpose "to get control, and to draw and to drain the Lakes that discharge their waters into the Wynants Kill, in a way that will make them most useful to the undersigned." About the same time, a ship basin and pier were built at the Poesten Kill's mouth (north along the west side of River Street) and the kill was channeled into a canal with a series of gates.

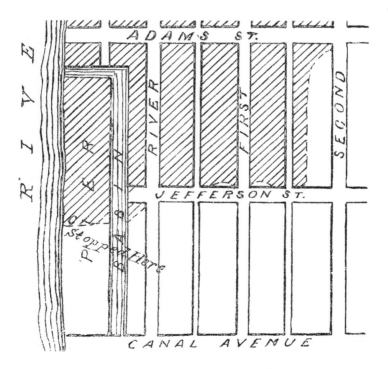

This map of the southern extent of the fire of 1854 also shows clearly the Poesten Kill Pier and Basin at the mouth of the kill; Canal Avenue is today's Ida Street along the Poesten Kill. *Courtesy Troy Public Library.*

"Improving" the Lower Poesten Kill

In the 1830s, there were still early raceways and millponds supplying the mills on the lower Poesten Kill, including a wooden one that brought water from along the cliffs in the upper reaches of Mill Street. A covered bridge at Spring Avenue spanned the kill below a millpond and by 1838 Canal Street (along the south bank of the Poesten Kill) had been constructed. The two "branches" of the Poesten Kill (stream and race) joined at the Hudson just below Hudson's Mill on Adams Street. This was the original site of Mahlon Taylor's lower gristmill and the raceway supplied its water power from a millpond at the junction of First and Adams Streets. A second millpond, which probably served Taylor's paper and lumber mills, was located at what was then a corner made by the end of Second and Jefferson Streets.

In 1834, Day Otis Kellogg estimated that the water power available on the Poesten Kill was barely being utilized and could support three dozen new water-powered mills and factories. Kellogg explained how he came to that conclusion:

> *The mill to which this estimate is applicable, is the flouring mill of four runs of stones, capable of grinding four runs of bushels per day. The Factory is the common cotton factory of average capacity, and supposed to require but half the power of the mill…The data for these calculations were obtained by actual admeasurements, taken in the month of August in that year* [1834]*, during one of the severest droughts with which this section of the country had been visited for many years. The maximum or even the ordinary average must be much greater.*

By 1835, the original Poesten Kill route was being drained and filled to make way for expansion of the city as Mahlon Taylor's northern raceway became the main channel between 1838 and 1845. Small sections of older waterworks survived into the 1870s, however. One was the north end of the Poesten Kill Ship Basin, which was being constructed at that time at the mouth of the kill. This block-wide lateral canal extended two blocks north of the Poesten Kill (nearly to Adams Street) a block from the Hudson River. Gates were installed in the new watercourse and the power was harnessed for the flouring and planing mills Taylor built nearby. The waterway was known alternately as the canal, the ship basin or the sloop lock, indicating its varied uses over the years. Another remnant of the old waterway was still visible into the 1880s. It was the large millpond that had been constructed on the Poesten Kill millrace near Third Street. Although a bridge crossed the Poesten Kill here, into the 1880s the sunken area of the old millpond had still not been filled. As a result, no homes were built on the block of Third Street north of the Poesten Kill to Madison Street until after 1890.

Much of the fill for the area around the Poesten Kill was taken from the foot of Mount Ida, and that, along with the brickworks at the base of the hill toward the north, led to a series of catastrophic landslides. There were certainly earlier slides lost to history, but the first reported in local papers occurred in 1836, when "a large mass of clay burst from the hill on the east section of the first ward [on the north side of the Poesten Kill]...followed by a gushing stream of water, and doing no other injury than covering a large portion of ground at the base with the bowels of the hill." During a snowstorm the following New Year's Day, a second, more damaging, slide took place. According to the *Troy Budget*, "An avalanche of clay came tumbling from an eminence of nearly five hundred feet, moving down the base of the hill to level land, and then continued...about 800 feet, covering up acres of ground, accompanied by a cataract of water and sand, which kept up a terrible roar." The slide destroyed two stables and three homes, "crushing them and their contents in thousands of pieces."

The slide carried four large trees down and hit the brick kiln, which lit the sky as it burned and caused the signal of "fire" to be given. When the rescuers arrived, the paper reported, "in the midst of a mass of convulsed earth, a multitude of human beings were moving to a fro, some carrying torches, and others digging among the ruins, and dragging from the midst the remains of some lifeless body...some were crying 'ho! ropes, ropes!' 'help!' 'shovels!' while the scene was dimly illuminated by the flames from the burning brick kiln." The bodies of John Grace and his wife Hannah were discovered in the ruins of his house, from which rescuers also pulled the Graces' young son, alive. Mrs. Leavenworth was taken from the ruins of her home battered and bruised but alive; her two children, Isaac (age eight) and Seaman (age four), were dead, "crushed almost to a jelly." Fortunately, the other members of the Leavenworth family were at church at the time the slide occurred.

Nine or ten "dirt carts" and twenty-two horses, no doubt being used to fill the area along the Poesten Kill, were carried by the slide into a hollow at the corner of Washington and Fourth Streets—just six horses survived. Their role in their own deaths was noted by the *Troy Budget*: "The clay is piled up in masses to the depth of from ten to forty feet," the paper noted, "it must have moved with great rapidity, and it is fortunate that it had not happened at the time when the laborers were employed digging from the hill…it's immediate cause is question of much speculation." Speculation as to the cause didn't stop the removal of soil from the base of Mount Ida, and the worst was not over. In 1840, two more small slides occurred, destroying a house from which the occupants escaped uninjured.

The most tragic slide occurred three years later in the same spot. The slide destroyed two houses immediately and then, as it went down Washington Street, all eight homes on both sides of the block; it finally came to rest just over Hill Street. "At the time of the slide," the *Troy Daily Whig* noted, "several men with teams were engaged at the bottom of the bank, carrying off earth." The paper also reported that the unnamed owner of the land "had frequently forbidden persons taking away the earth from the hill, being fearful of a catastrophe like that which happened. But his orders were disregarded and the consequence has been the loss of life to fifteen human beings." Ten years later, another landslide occurred, this one on the south side of the Poesten Kill, east of Fourth Street (behind the old India rubber shoe factory), and the wife and three children of Patrick Martin narrowly escaped drowning when their house and several cows were swept away. Their house stood on the opposite (north) bank of the Poesten Kill on what is now Ida Street. The *Whig* noted that "as the slide reached the creek it forced the water over the road taking with it the house, with one woman, three children, and several cows."

The landslides of 1836, 1837 and 1843 apparently had no effect on those wishing to build on the slope of Mount Ida north of the Poesten Kill. In 1858, a cornerstone was laid close to the hill for the new St. Peter's College, a project of Reverend Peter Havermans, the pastor of St. Mary's Church. Nearly $15,000 had been spent and the building's second floor was being built when the hill behind the building gave way and it was all but destroyed on St. Patrick's Day 1859. Amazingly, the *Daily Whig* called it "a terrible avalanche—from which our city has been free for many years."

"The College was located upon a large plateau, to which the approach was by a broad flight of steps," the writer declared. "It was the highest building in that vicinity and nearest the hill. Below it, at the base of the steps are a number of houses upon Washington Street. The building was intended to be a very large one, 200 feet in length and five stories high, with two towers." St. Patrick's Day then being a holiday, the more than one hundred workmen were not on the scene. Had the building not stopped it, it's believed that the slide would have reached the southwest corner of Washington and Fifth Streets, where the first Troy Hospital had stood. The hospital was on the site of a long-standing orphanage run by St. Mary's Roman Catholic Church. As the hill remained in a dangerous state for some time, those with homes at the bottom were forced to clear out, as was the orphanage.

FLOURING, GRAIN
AND GRISTMILLS

Gristmill production on the Poesten Kill was significantly enlarged by the mill of Moses Vail, built in 1794 above Mahlon Taylor's near the bridge at Spring Avenue. Vail was a merchant and politician from Nassau who symbolized like few others the value of the Poesten Kill mill properties. Before moving to Troy, Vail had served in the New York State Assembly, and after moving to Troy he was elected a member of the New York State Senate; he also served as Rensselaer County sheriff. One of his sons, George Vail, was first president of both the Merchants' and Mechanics' Bank and the Rensselaer County Agricultural Society, as well as an early president of the State Agricultural Society and a personal friend of Presidents Andrew Jackson and Martin Van Buren and New York governor William L. Marcy. Henry Vail, another son of Moses, was a congressman who purchased the River-View estate of Albert P. Heartt on the summit of Mount Ida.

Moses Vail's son-in-law Townsend McCoun (president and chairman of the Troy Savings Bank when it was incorporated in 1823) operated the mill from as early as 1816 and into the 1830s, when the firm became known as Vail & Hayner and was operated by Joseph Vail, who passed it to his son Townsend McCoun Vail. According to Cuyler Reynolds's *Hudson-Mohawk Genealogical and Family Memoirs*, Townsend M. Vail "succeeded his father as head of the business [then called Globe Mills] which was carried on most successfully until freight rates and a decreased supply of home grown wheat made the business less profitable." Townsend Vail was also heavily connected to the growth of Troy. He was a director, trustee and second vice-president of the Troy Savings Bank and heavily promoted the building of the Troy Savings Bank Music Hall. He was also a director of the Troy and Boston Railroad, the Congress Street Bridge Company and the Troy Gaslight Company.

The Vails' prestige was rivaled by that of Mahlon Taylor, who owned about one hundred acres along the Poesten Kill by 1800. Mahlon Taylor's new gristmill was located on his raceway near the mouth of the Poesten Kill and is believed to have been the first in the area with a mechanical elevator. It was later also fitted out for the milling of plaster by Benjamin Taylor in 1803. In 1809, Benjamin Taylor advertised the sale of this grist- and plaster mill and described it as having "two run of burrs, both turned at the same time by the same water wheel." By 1825, the milling of grain was the primary industry along the Poesten Kill, with some 325,000 bushels of wheat being milled into flour that year. Storehouses along the river were then four and five stories high, with large basements. Wheat, rye, corn and other grains were brought in on wagons and sleighs and hoisted into the upper floors, where they were weighed and dumped into bins. These cribs had chutes at the bottom that were opened directly into vessels on the docks below. Approximately $2.5 million worth of goods was shipped from Troy in 1825, much of it grain products, and by the 1830s grain and other goods arriving from the north and west of Troy outpaced by far that which came from the countryside to the east.

One milling company that heavily relied on shipping its product far and wide was that of Oliver Boutwell at the mouth of the Poesten Kill. Boutwell began a bakery on River Street in 1831 and moved to Grand Division Street in 1833. In 1836–37, he turned the bakery over to his brother, Phardice Boutwell, and began milling grain, flour and feed from the improved Poesten Kill. Beginning with a two-story mill, he eventually occupied two hundred feet along River Street with machinery operated by wheels on the Poesten Kill Basin. The firm was one of the larger flouring mills in Troy in the 1800s, and from his offices on the north side of the mill Boutwell managed the milling of wheat, corn, rye and oats next door. At the complex's south end, Nova Scotia plaster was ground and there was a large storehouse with four elevators. Boutwell mill's product was

Flouring, Grain and Gristmills

Andrew Ruff owned and operated this mill on Hill Street until 1929, one of the longest running gristmills on the Poesten Kill. The last of his mill buildings, part of the older Loveland Crissey & Company's Canal Mills (at left), was destroyed by fire in 1968. *Courtesy Troy Public Library.*

loaded for shipping onto watercraft in the ship basin at the rear of the mills and railroad cars at the front. The mill was lucky to have survived the fire of 1854, although one of its newer mill buildings was destroyed by fire in April 1890; it was replaced later that year by a four-story structure. When the first regular freight train went through the Hoosac Tunnel in April 1875, it was primarily loaded with wheat from the Boutwell Mills bound for J. Cushing & Co. of Fitchburg, Massachusetts. Boutwell's son Charles joined the firm in 1866, and when his father died in 1888 he took over until its bankruptcy in 1904, long after the death of the flouring industry in Troy more generally. Token coins from the Boutwell Mills from the 1830s until the Civil War are said to have turned up as pennies in Troy change drawers into the 1940s.

THE IDA HILL
NEIGHBORHOOD

Congress Street was one of the earliest roads in Rensselaer County because it provided the easiest access to the interior of the county from the Hudson River. Beginning on the east bank of the Hudson, it winds its way up a long, abandoned branch of the Poesten Kill past Mount Ida to the kill at what is now Pawling Avenue. Mount Ida was named for the Hellenic Mount Ida that overlooked classical Troy. A second, smaller hill to the north was once called Mount Olympus. Initially, the Mount Ida neighborhood was used for recreation, cemeteries, farms (such as that of John Fonda) and later the summer homes of Troy's wealthiest residents, most notably those of the Warren and Vail families (at what is now Prospect Park), George Tibbits and Samuel Wilson. A few other homes were scattered along Congress Street, and an early 1830s Greek Revival cottage still stands at 541 Congress. Mount Ida Cemetery was the city's primary cemetery until the mid-1800s.

In the 1830s, the grist- and sawmills below the falls were dominant and as late as 1845 the area above the Vail Mill was still generally undeveloped. The transformation of Ida Hill into an industrial powerhouse can be said to have begun with Benjamin Marshall. As a young man, Marshall, with his brother Joseph, was a cotton importer in New York City. With his friend Francis Thompson, Marshall enjoyed a more than twenty-year career shipping Georgia cotton to England and returning with finished goods. Marshall spent his winters in Georgia and there became friends and business associates with the cotton planter Nicholas Turnbull. Following the

The Ida Hill Neighborhood

interruption of shipping during the War of 1812, Marshall, along with Francis and Jeremiah Thompson and Isaac Wright, organized what has been said to be the first regular packet ship line—the Black Ball Line—between New York and Liverpool. In 1825, Marshall divested himself from the shipping business and with his brother Joseph and Benjamin Wolcott built two cotton factories. The first, known as New York Mills, was outside Utica and became perhaps the largest cotton mill complex outside New England in the 1830s. The second was the Hudson Print Works and Mt. Ida Cotton Mill on the Poesten Kill, also known as Ida Mills; he later purchased cotton mills in Middlebury, Vermont, and North Adams, Massachusetts.

Ida Mills was one of the largest operations on the entire Poesten Kill, and in 1830 the Troy city directory reported on its capacity:

> The Ida Mills—*This establishment is for spinning and weaving cotton. It contains 2,400 spindles, and 68 power looms; spins 55,000 lbs. yarn, nos. 32 to 36, and 20,000 lbs yarn, nos. 5 to 20, per annum; weaves 270,000 yards cotton cloth from the fine yarn, most of which is printed at the Hudson print works; employs about 100 hands, a majority being females and children. About 170 persons derive their support from the establishment. A day school is kept in the precincts throughout the year, and a night school about half the year.*

In 1840, Marshall designed and constructed a dam and power canal. First the Poesten Kill was dammed at the east end of the gorge (just below Pawling Avenue). Then an intake was built on the north side of the Poesten Kill behind the dam. From there, Marshall had a six-hundred-foot-long tunnel cut to supply his mill. Later, a turbine connected to an electric generator at the system's lower end supplied electrical power until 1962, when it went off line. Recently a new hydroelectric system was built using some of the original 1840 power canal system. The success of Benjamin Marshall's mills led him to build housing for his millworkers on the Poesten Kill's south side, along with the Marshall Infirmary for the Insane in 1851. Ida Mills was later occupied by a succession of companies and was torn down in the early 1980s.

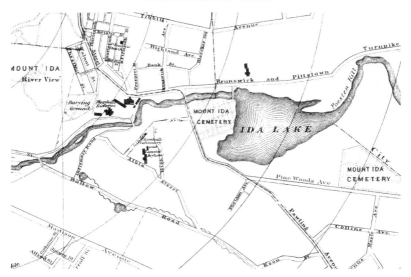

This 1880 map of the Ida Hill Neighborhood shows an enlarged Ida Lake and bridges over the Poesten Kill below the Marshall Mills, at the junction of Hollow Road (later Spring Avenue), and at Pawling Avenue where the Troy and Albia Horse Railroad Company crosses. *Courtesy Troy Public Library.*

Above Marshall's mills, another race was built, on which William R. Yourt erected a bleach works. Yourt, who came to America from Ireland in the 1820s, had been an associate of Benjamin Marshall in New York Mills. He purchased much of the old Fonda farm along both sides of the Poesten Kill from Pawling Avenue east and established his home on the corner of Pawling and Linden Avenues. In 1859, the original bleach works was destroyed by fire; the main building was completely destroyed, but the storehouse, containing several thousands of dollars worth of goods, and the nearby drying house were saved. The main works were rebuilt and operated by Yourt and Marshall, and later the Franklin Farnam's Excelsior Hosiery Mill; the dam was replaced in 1912 and lasted until 1997. The Bleach Works Pond became known in the 1870s as Ida Lake and later Belden Pond, once a very popular ice-skating spot.

Franklin Farnam was a Massachusetts dry goods and grocery merchant who settled in Cohoes in the 1840s. In 1852, he and partners established a factory for making linen thread from American flax. Farnam's operation was moved to the north side of the Poesten Kill, named Excelsior Knitting Mill and by the end of the Civil War was manufacturing hosiery day and night. In 1884, the mill was renamed the Crown Knitting Mills of the Brunswick Manufacturing Company. The Crown Mills produced fine wool products for women and children, along with merino (fine wool) hosiery and cotton underwear.

Farnam and his wife found an interest in the mission work of St. John's (Troy's second Episcopal church, founded in 1830) at the corner of Liberty and First Streets, the mixed industrial and residential neighborhood on the north side of the Poesten Kill. St. John's rector, George H. Walsh, organized the St. John's Free Mission to minister to the workers in the mills on Ida Hill. The first meeting brought together forty-four people at a local home, but soon the small congregation was meeting in a room in a building behind the Ida Mills cotton factory and later in homes near the top of the hill on Congress Street's south side. In short order, the Farnams determined to build the Free Church of the Ascension, and the cornerstone was laid in October 1869. The church cost the Farnams personally about $45,000, including a large stained-glass window and a set of nine bells. Built in gothic style in the shape of a cross of blue and free stone with a 106-foot tower rising over the Poesten Kill High Falls, it still stands on the north side of Congress Street. Once the church was on its feet, the Farnams contributed another $25,000 for a parish school and meeting hall across the street, the Farnam Institute, built in 1872.

Franklin Farnam was also instrumental in reorganizing the local fire department. The first on Ida Hill was Lafayette Engine Company No. 10, organized in 1839. The old company was becoming obsolete with the introduction of steam engines, so Farnam revitalized it in 1871 and it took the name F.W. Farnam Steam-Engine Company No. 5. Farnam purchased a new steam engine from L. Button & Son in Waterford and had a new brick engine house built on the south side of Congress Street in 1876 alongside the kill (a second Button steamer was acquired by Farnam in 1885). The Farnam firehouse was converted to apartments in the 1910s and was destroyed by fire in 1970. The company played a

Workers used this bridge in the gorge to reach the mills on the Poesten Kill's north side from their homes on the south side. The Free Church of the Ascension is in plain view; left of the church is the F.W. Farnam Steam-Engine Company No. 5, and just beyond, the steeple of the Farnam Institute on the north side of Congress Street. *Courtesy Poestenkill Historical Society.*

significant role in the Ida Hill neighborhood and several leading citizens were members.

Marshall's textile factory began the blossoming of related businesses on Ida Hill. All along Congress Street, dozens of retail establishments were founded to supply local residents with their needs. Businesses based on textiles also exploded around the city and into the towns above. Hannah Lord Montague is credited with inventing the detachable collar in 1827, and in the early 1830s Orlando Montague and Austin Granger began making detachable linen collars and shirt fronts, or "dickeys," in a factory setting, initiating an industry that earned Troy the nickname "Collar City." Even though it got a later start than the local iron industry, by 1860 the manufacture of shirts, collars and cuffs was the largest industry in Troy, employing nearly five thousand workers, mostly women. By 1923, some ten thousand workers were employed producing $43 million worth of collars and cuffs.

THE LOWER
POESTEN KILL GORGE

O ne of the unique features of manufacturing along the Poesten
Kill in the 1800s was its diversity. Leather, wool, flax, cotton,
silk, paper, rags, rope, wood, rubber, clay, sand, ore, zinc, lead, iron,
steel, charcoal and coal were just some of the raw materials used in
the making of textiles and garments, iron and steel products, paper
and paint, brick, boots and cotton batten along the kill. In 1845,
there were some 320 factory and millworkers on the kill in Troy
alone, more than three times the number employed in the rest of
Troy's factories and mills.

Below the Marshall Factories stood Manning Paper's Mount Ida
Mill, the longest-operating factory on the kill. The Mount Ida paper
mill was founded in 1845 by William Manning, Gardner Howland
(owner of the paper mill in Cropseyville) and Alvin Williams to
make paper from recycled Manila hemp rope (mostly for use as
flour sacks, wrapping paper and envelopes). The following year,
they built a large mill at the foot of Cypress Street using water
power from the Marshall Power Tunnel. In the late 1800s, under
the direction of William's son John A. Manning, the company was
the largest maker of paper from Manila hemp in the world. The
younger Manning established larger paper mills on River Street
after the Civil War. In 1903, Manning became the country's first
unionized paper company before moving some of the facilities to
the old Gilbert Car Works on Green Island in 1915. The Mount
Ida plant, however, operated until 1962, when it burned down and
its operations were transferred to Green Island. Family control of

the company ended when it was purchased by Hammerill in 1970, and in 1986, Manning was purchased by Lydall; the Green Island plant still produces thermal and flame barriers, electrical insulating and cryogenic super-insulating materials.

Below Manning on the kill at the foot of Cypress Street was the Griswold Wire Works, which included various companies over the years. The J. Wool Griswold Company manufactured iron; Bessemer steel; bright, galvanized and cooper wire; bale ties; nails; and staples beginning in 1879, after John Wool Griswold's departure as superintendent of the Bessemer Steel Mill. In the 1890s, it began manufacturing a number of barbed wires of its own design with names like Griswold's Flyer, Side Lock, Folded Wing and Griswold's Savage. The Brockner-Evans Company made steel bale ties in the facility until 1884, when that work was taken over by Griswold Brothers (John Wool Griswold and Frank B. Griswold, the sons of congressman and former Troy mayor John A. Griswold and grandnephews of General John Wool). All told, the mill could make three thousand tons of wire a year with 133 wire drawing blocks, but it was much smaller than a second wire mill that J. Wool Griswold owned with W.M. Dillon in Sterling, Illinois, which was formed in 1893. William Hamilton Shields, the mill's former manager, took over the Troy Griswold Wire works around 1900, and the works closed in 1911.

The Tompkins works produced knitting machinery just west of Griswold Brothers. Its factory was supplied by a millpond with a fall of twenty-five feet that provided seventy-five horsepower. Weise reports that Clark Tompkins (from Rhode Island by way of Cohoes) built a brick factory to make mill gearing, looms for cotton and carpet mills and general machinery about 1846. The original building was destroyed by fire in 1849 and replaced the following year. Clark Tompkins initially had partners with whom he organized the Empire Machine Company, which produced a highly popular upright rotary knitting machine invented by Tompkins and distributed throughout the country, Canada and South America. Tompkins served as superintendent of the new company until 1861, when he became the company's sole owner. In 1877, Tompkins's sons, Ira and Albert, took over the company

The Lower Poesten Kill Gorge

From 1879 until 1911, the Griswold Wire Works at the foot of Cypress Street could make three thousand tons a year of iron; steel; and bright, galvanized and cooper wire; along with staples and nails. *Courtesy Troy Public Library.*

and renamed it Tompkins Brothers. Tompkins Brothers moved to Syracuse in 1919 and continued to make knitting machines until it went out of business in 2006.

The Brookside Hosiery Mills, begun in 1872, was also located at the foot of Cypress Street. In 1880, William C. Tompkins (brother to the Tompkins brothers above) took over the company, which made "cotton, woolen, and merino shirts; drawers, pantalets, and union suits." William Tompkins made the papers frequently in the 1880s after he divorced his wife Lizzie and began shacking up with the comedic vaudeville actress Myra Goodwin in the fall of 1883. Tompkins sold the mills for $50,000, apparently to produce the play *Sis*, written especially for Goodwin. It opened in 1885 at the Fourteenth Street Theatre in Manhattan and also played in Boston, but it closed the following year due, it was reported,

West of the Griswold Wire Works was the Tompkins Brothers machine works, which produced a highly popular upright rotary knitting machine distributed throughout the country, Canada and South America. The company moved to Syracuse in 1919 and continued to make knitting machines until it went out of business in 2006. *Courtesy Troy Public Library.*

to Goodwin's poor health. In 1887, Tompkins was arrested for trying to skip out on a $10,000 debt; he died in West Troy at the age of fifty-six in 1894.

Another important business on the lower Poesten Kill was William Connors's "paint and color works" between Ida and Hill Streets, which produced roof paints, stove cement, steam putty, white lead, zinc and ready mixed paints "from pint to a barrel of any desired color." Today a parking lot stands in its location. Nearby was a company owned by Jonas S. Heartt, onetime mayor of Troy, who teamed with fire brick maker James Ostrander in 1856 to form the Troy Fire Brick Works. After the Civil War, Heartt went his own way and established the Jonas S. Heartt & Company, manufacturing train car wheels at the corner of Ida and Second Streets from 1867 to 1894. James Ostrander continued with the Troy Fire Brick Works, adding his son Francis to the firm in 1868. Their works took up twenty-seven lots between First and Second Streets from Canal Avenue to Madison Street on the Poesten Kill's south side. Using clay and sand that the company mined in Woodbridge, New Jersey, and kaolin from Staten Island, the works made a variety of shapes and sizes of fire brick, block and tile from three pounds to one hundred for use in cook and parlor stove linings, furnaces, forges, foundries and factories. The approximately one hundred workers at the works produced the first fire brick used in the Bessemer plant. In 1874, Francis Ostrander took over the company at the death of his father, and the company closed in the late 1920s; the offices of the brick works were on Second Street.

THE IRON AND
STEEL INDUSTRIES

One of the most common elements on earth today, iron is also the most widely used of all metals, and its low cost and high strength made it indispensable to the industrial age. The Poesten Kill was well positioned to become an industrial center that rivaled traditional iron and steel towns like Pittsburgh. Thanks to its location, Troy foundries (and those in Eagle Mills) could easily supply their needs for the production of iron and iron products. The Adirondacks was one of ten principal iron ore–producing regions in America and, by way of the Champlain Canal, the major supplier of the area's iron ore, along with Duchess and Columbia Counties. Charcoal and lumber used to fire the furnaces was cut in the mountains of eastern Rensselaer County, which still held plenty of timber in the mid-1800s. Limestone for flux came from the Helderbergs in eastern Albany County, and molding sand (important for casting) from around the region. Finished goods were in turn shipped around the country along the canal, river and rail systems. Ploughs and farming implements, household goods, tools, kettles, stoves, structural and ornamental architecture and industrial uses such as machinery parts, cauldrons and more were produced all along the Poesten Kill; school, church and farm bells all along the kill were made in the foundries in and around Troy.

Iron was produced in either blast furnaces or forges, and both required a large amount of fuel. Until the late 1800s, when coal began to supplant its use, that typically meant charcoal. Colliers (charcoal makers) from the eastern hill towns did a brisk business

The Iron and Steel Industries

supplying the iron manufacturers in Troy, where several major foundries stood. The Marshall Foundry was built by Charles Kellogg about 1850 at the corner of Fifteenth Street on Ida Hill. Kellogg produced specialized drills and presses, boring and mortising machines, portable forges, currycombs and a variety of hardware items from window blinds to percussion caps. Also about 1850, George Harrison and William Knight built the Troy Malleable Iron foundry on the north side of Congress Street, between Marshall and Christie Streets. The architectural ironworks foundry of Michael Mahoney and Calvin W. Link (Troy Architectural Irons Works & Foundry) made machinery castings and ornamental building materials on the south side of Spring Avenue beginning in 1870; another foundry on Spring Avenue was that of Hoyt & Wynkoop. On the lower Poesten Kill on the corner of Ida and Second Streets was the Empire Stove Foundry, built about 1840, and below that the enormous Rensselaer Iron Works and Clinton Foundries stood on the Hudson, south of the kill. A foundry also existed in Eagle Mills.

The iron industry began locally with the mills of John Brinkerhoff (1807) and John Converse (1809) on the Wynants Kill. Brinkerhoff used wrought iron to produce nail rods and hoop iron on the site that would become the Albany Rolling and Slitting Mill. Soon, other iron-related businesses sprang up; one of the earliest, in 1818, was established by Nathaniel and Charles Starbuck as the Troy Plough Factory (whose products were popular throughout the county). In 1821, the Troy Air Furnace began casting machinery parts, kettles and cauldrons and, more importantly, stoves for Starbuck & Gurley, another important industry along the Poesten Kill. The first stove foundry may have been established as early as 1812 and some two hundred other firms over the years were associated with the stove industry, making patterns, building stoves from stove plate made at outside foundries or selling stoves to the wholesale and/or retail markets. By 1830, there were several stove foundries in Troy, and by 1845 about a half dozen companies were making some thirty-five thousand stoves a year. Less than ten years later, nearly seven hundred workers made more than twice that number, including the most popular, designed by Philo Penfield

Ploughs and farming implements, household goods, tools, kettles, stoves, structural and ornamental architecture and iron products for industrial uses were all produced along the Poesten Kill. Delee & Hayes on Congress Street, Ida Hill, made springs for carriages and wagons. *Courtesy Troy Public Library.*

Stewart, better known as a founder of Oberlin Colony and Oberlin College. Stewart was a mechanic, teacher, missionary, abolitionist, reformer and philanthropist. Although born in Connecticut and educated in Vermont, Stewart invented an improved cookstove design in New York City before moving to Troy in order to partner with a manufacturer. He joined first with Starbuck & Company, which had begun making stoves in 1821. He then joined the firm of Fuller, Warren & Company (Joseph Fuller and Walter P. Warren), where he perfected a design that helped make that company the leading stove maker into the late 1800s.

By the late 1870s, there were twenty-three companies employing more than 2,000 workers making close to 200,000 stoves a year. "A man who cannot suit himself with a stove in walking along River-street, Troy, must be one of those creatures—too often to be met—impossible to please," the *New York Times* declared

The Iron and Steel Industries

in 1872, for "he could pick and choose between base-burners, self-feeders, gas-consumers, patent bakers, hot closets, reservoirs, and a hundred other sorts." Among the largest of Troy's stove foundries was Fuller & Warren's Clinton Stove Works. It was built in 1846 by Johnson and Cox at the foot of Monroe Street, just south of the Poesten Kill below the mills of the Rensselaer Iron Works. The works covered some five or six acres, with several buildings four to six stories high, and employed more than 1,200 workers making 60,000 stoves a year from forty tons of iron a day. It was one of Troy's largest foundries and the site of numerous labor strikes. The company had large salesrooms in New York City, Boston, Cleveland and Chicago and built another large foundry in Milwaukee. The Troy foundry closed in 1932 and the last Troy stove company, Burdett, Smith & Co., closed its doors in 1936. The few remaining buildings of the Clinton Works were torn down in 1998; it is now the site of Bruno Machinery.

The most intact remnant of the stove foundries is the four-story building on the north side of the Poesten Kill facing Second Street, which was once part of the Empire Foundry. The facilities once stretched along the Poesten Kill, where a three-story building housed the fitting and mounting operations. The building was used for storage and office space until about 1920, when it was the home of Lindy's Hardware (until 1999). Built about 1840, the Empire Foundry was initially powered by water (later steam) from the Poesten Kill supplied by the old millpond at Second Street and was home to at least ten companies before it became the Empire Stove Works. Across Ida Street stood the foundry itself, with two cupola furnaces along the south side of the molding shop. At its height in the 1870s, the company employed some two hundred men producing stoves worth $500,000 a year. In January 1902, the main foundry building was destroyed by fire. At the time, it housed the Mount Ida Nickel Works and scale manufacturer James Hislop, who was still putting the old foundry to use under the name National Foundry.

In October 1845, LeGrand B. Cannon purchased several lots on the south side of the Poesten Kill between the kill and Madison Avenue. In the spring of the following year, the Troy Vulcan

The Kellogg factory on Ida Hill was one of a number of area firms producing iron products along the Poesten Kill. Over the years, this factory produced specialized drills and presses, boring and mortising machines, portable forges, currycombs and a variety of hardware items, from window blinds to percussion caps. *Courtesy Troy Public Library.*

Company (of which Cannon was a trustee) built a large rolling mill there, the first of its kind in Troy. The mill went through several owners before the Civil War as the Troy Rolling Mill Company became the Rensselaer Iron Company in the 1850s. Later, the Rensselaer Iron Works, then under the ownership of John A. Griswold & Co., was devoted to rolling steel and iron rails and bars and manufacturing iron for other uses. In 1870, a second building, known as the rail mill, was built on the north side of the Poesten Kill. Both mills on the Poesten Kill rolled ingots supplied by the Bessemer steel plant nearby. In 1875, Rensselaer Iron Works was consolidated with the Albany Iron Works on the Wynants Kill and together became known as the Albany and Rensselaer Iron Works and Steel Company, with Erastus Corning as president. The consolidation made the Troy iron and steel industries preeminent in America. In the 1870s, the various mills and furnaces were powered by thirty-five steam engines and the water mills provided

The Iron and Steel Industries

This unusual 1886 view looking west at the Rensselaer Iron Company's rolling mill (at left) and rail mill also shows the Troy & Greenbush Railroad line in the foreground, the train having just crossed the bridge over the Poesten Kill at River Street. *Courtesy Troy Public Library.*

five hundred horsepower to aid the work of nearly two thousand workers; the facilities used some 120,000 tons of coal to produce 90,000 tons of iron and steel.

Troy's iron and steel industries also spurred the making and machining of parts and specialized equipment along the Poesten Kill. Jonas Phelps and William Gurley became leading makers of precision surveying instruments. The Gurley instrument company produced telescopes, compasses, clocks, transits, plane tables, levels, chains, rods and drawing instruments that were shipped to such faraway places as Asia, the Middle East and South and Central America. George M. Phelps learned the machine trade at Phelps and Gurley as a mathematical instrument maker and set up his own shop in 1850 at the corner of First and Adams Streets making light-duty machinery, safe locks, paper-sorting machines and eventually a popular brand of printing telegraphs. George Phelps designed the ball that dropped each day at Times Square's Western Union building, allowing city residents to accurately set their watches. Another prominent specialized machine shop was that founded by George Ross in 1879; the Ross Valve Company is now in its sixth generation.

The Ludlow Valve Company was established by Henry Ludlow of Nassau in 1861. He began the company in Waterford but moved to Lansingburgh in 1872 and then into the facilities of the Rensselaer Iron Company in 1897. Ludlow breathed new life into the old mills on the Poesten Kill. It was the largest valve maker and fire hydrant maker in the world and had close associations with RPI. Following

The lower Poesten Kill was once crowded with industrial buildings. Troy residents hope a riverfront "Artifact Park" here will connect with Prospect Park via a walkway along the Poesten Kill. *Courtesy Rensselaer County Historical Society.*

World War II, the company's business began to wane, and a merger with Rensselaer Valve Company in 1954 could not stem the tide. In the 1960s, foreclosure was begun and the plant ended production in 1969. Today, however, Ludlow valves are still made under the Patterson Pump Company name in Georgia.

Ludlow, Ross and Gurley were notable exceptions, but by the late 1870s the local iron and steel industries were beginning to wane as plants moved to the coal-producing regions in the West and the United States Steel Corporation consolidated the industry. The rolling mill building survived until recent years and was used by the scrap metal recycling company Scholite Products until the late 1990s; the property went into foreclosure and was bought by the city in 2001. In May 2008, an arsonist's fire broke out there and the next day it was unceremoniously demolished. Troy hopes to replace the old mill building with a riverfront "Artifact Park" that will connect with Prospect Park via a walkway along the Poesten Kill. Beside the park, the Beacon Institute has proposed a $15 million River and Estuaries Center.

ALONG THE UPPER POESTEN KILL

Initially, life along the upper Poesen Kill in the villages of Eagle Mills, Cropseyville (named for Valentine Cropsey), Poestenkill, Barberville and East Poestenkill (once called Columbia) depended on the natural resources available there. Potash, furs, lumber and charcoal were the most important products on the upper Poesten Kill into the late 1800s. Potash had been used since antiquity in the making of soap, glass, dyeing and fertilizer, and it provided the earliest settlers with needed cash and credit as they cleared woodlands in order to plant crops. Excess hardwood, including stumps, was burned and the ashes carefully saved and then leached with water to make lye. The lye was then boiled down in large kettles and dried by evaporation to produce the potash, also known as "black salts." An acre of hardwoods could produce sixty to one hundred bushels of potash, which brought anywhere from three to six dollars a bushel—about the same rate laborers were paid to clear woodlands.

Women and children (and some men) along the upper Poesten Kill also took part in a vibrant industry of forest and field products. Blackberries, blueberries, raspberries and huckleberries were picked and crated for sale in Troy. Cherry bark was carefully peeled and dried for use in cough syrups and other medicinals, and sugar bushes were tapped for maple syrup. Christmas trees and wreaths were produced in mountain shacks around small stoves in winter, where balsam boughs and princess and ground pine were also wound into holiday roping. Barrel hoops made from the flexible

People living in East Poestenkill, the largest community in the upper reaches of the Poesten Kill, primarily made their livings from forest products, logging and charcoal production. *Courtesy Poestenkill Historical Society.*

gray birch were split and shaped with a drawing knife. "Mouth root," an early mouthwash, was gathered, dried and packed for Troy to be used in the production of bitter tonics. One of the most productive and valuable forest products was ferns. Two types, "fancy" and "dagger," were gathered during the "fern season" in August and September and bundled for shipment by local packers and shippers. Charles Beck from Sand Lake would drive his wagon to East Poestenkill to meet the fern pickers as they came out of the woods. Beck packed each bunch loosely, sprinkled them with water and layered them with moss and paper in boxes ready to be shipped to florists throughout the East. Ferns were in high demand and brought a price of thirty-five cents per thousand during the 1930s and two dollars per thousand in 1958. If the supply was plentiful, it was said that a picker could bring in ten thousand ferns a day.

Local farmers and then professional loggers worked to strip the surrounding forests. Among them were French Canadians who continued to live near East Poestenkill long after the logging industry had run its course. Crude lumber camps were located in the mountains east of East Poestenkill, and early millers in that area included James Henderson (Poestenkill's first elected supervisor)

Along the Upper Poesten Kill

and James Rogers at Roger's Bridge, a community now long gone. Little is known about the majority of sawmills along the highest reaches of the Poesten Kill, but early sawmills were also located on the kill's steeper stretches in East Poestenkill (then called Columbia), at Barberville, at Eagle Mills and on the Quacken Kill at Rock Hollow (East Brunswick) and Cropseyville.

Before 1900, there were nearly twenty lumber mills along the uppermost reaches of the Poesten Kill, many with sizable millponds. The dams for millponds were typically built with cribbing of large logs and stone. A simple lock system using planks was devised to control the flow of water onto the mill's overshot wheel. As late as the 1980s, the remains of some of these dams could still be seen, notably at the abandoned millpond just east of Poestenkill Village on Plank Road. For many years the old Plank Road millpond was a popular swimming hole known as "Board Bottom." This was the site of the earliest sawmill at Poesten Kill Village, believed to have been that of Christian Cooper (in the late 1700s it may have been operated by Peter Cooper). George H. Cooper took over his father's mill and it was later owned by George Borst, John Holser and finally Albert Schumann. Later a steam-operated portable mill was hauled around the countryside by John and Lewis Miller. Other notable sawyers along the upper Poesten Kill included Henry Milhizer (at East Poestenkill), Peleg Mason, David Cipperly, Garret Ives, George Cottrell and P.G. Hayner.

Local factories, particularly the glass works in Sand Lake and the iron furnaces and forges in Troy, required a large amount of fuel. Until the late 1800s, when coal began to supplant its use, that typically meant charcoal and cordwood. Colliers (charcoal makers) along the mountainous reaches of Poesten Kill did a brisk business supplying the iron manufacturers in Troy with their rattling high-sided wagons. Every ton of iron required some three to five hundred bushels of charcoal, and two and a quarter cords of hardwood were needed to produce one hundred bushels. Colliers made their charcoal using large pits or beehive constructions in which a fire was started and the entire pile of wood was sealed to keep out most of the air; later, stone and brick buildings were constructed. Hardwood logging for charcoal manufacture probably far outpaced

Before 1900 there were nearly twenty lumber mills along the uppermost reaches of the Poesten Kill, many with sizable millponds held back by dams made of a cribbing of large logs and stone. This one near Poestenkill Village was one of the few that were improved with concrete. *Courtesy Poestenkill Historical Society.*

lumbering, particularly with beech, birch and maple. Pine and then spruce were generally turned into merchantable lumber, which was used locally and sold to the saw- and planing mills along the Poesten Kill. Mills all along the Poesten Kill provided lumber for the boom in construction throughout the county that occurred before the Civil War. In addition to marketable lumber, kindling and cordwood for general heating were also taken. Heavy timbers from oak were used for docks and wharves at Troy, and later for telephone, telegraph and electric utility poles. In the late 1800s, pulp wood was supplied to the paper mills at Troy and Mechanicsville and ash was taken to the furniture makers as far as Vermont. A byproduct of lumbering—sawdust—was collected from the mills for use on slippery floors in butcher shops and slaughterhouses, and for packing ice into the region's many icehouses.

Along the Upper Poesten Kill

Hemlock was cut for its bark, which was used in tanning. The bark was ground and leached to provide tannin to turn cowhides into shoes, boots and other leather products. In local tanneries, large vats were made by digging deep rectangular pits and were lined with hemlock planks that extended above ground. A large number of "green hides" were shipped from as far away as South America for processing. John Beals operated a tan yard in the village of Poestenkill until 1814, when it was destroyed by a flood; the town of Brunswick also had a tannery before 1815. The largest tannery on the Poesten Kill was the Haight tannery in Troy. Samuel B. Haight began running a tannery on the kill's south side near Spring Avenue in 1839 and the Haight family soon became a preeminent name in the industry. The elder Haight son, Samuel, established his own large tannery in Milton, Saratoga County, in 1870, just three years before the old family tannery near the kill was destroyed by fire. In 1880, another son, H.B. Haight, took over the former flour mill site of Mahlon Taylor on Hill Street, and by 1885 the buildings extended 150 feet along both sides of the kill and employed one hundred workers who tanned twenty-five thousand hides a year. Because large tanneries used thousands of cords of bark a year, the hemlock was quickly depleted in the upper Poesten Kill, and the local tanneries were fairly short-lived there. In the early 1840s, Brunswick had two tanneries of its own, but by 1860 there were just two tanneries in both towns. One was on the Quacken Kill in Cropseyville and the other, the tannery of Nicholas Taylor in Poestenkill Village, employed two men producing about two thousand hides a year. By the 1890s, the tanning industry was consolidated on the southern tier of New York and in the west, and it had all but disappeared along the Poesten Kill by 1900.

Grain, feed and flouring mills were also well established on the upper Poesten Kill. An early miller operated at Poestenkill Village on the Back Street raceway, and later a gristmill was located at the Cooper sawmill and operated in conjunction with it. A similar situation held in Cropseyville, where Paul Smith operated a joint saw- and gristmill before 1809. The Cropsey family operated a gristmill between 1810 and 1866, but the largest early gristmill was the four-story brick Eagle Flouring Mill built by Daniel Sheldon in

This grist- and sawmill on Plank Road in Poestenkill Village operated into the twentieth century. Initially it used water power from the Poesten Kill but was later powered by a steam engine. *Courtesy Poestenkill Historical Society.*

1821 on the west side of the Poesten Kill at what is now Eagle Mills. A drop of twenty-five feet provided the power for the Eagle Mill (and a number of other businesses in the village) to allow the milling of local grain into Eagle Brand Flour. The Eagle Mill was later operated by James Burnstead, who milled feed from local grains. By then the millers in Troy were coming into their ascendency; the Burnstead mill didn't last long before it was put to work in the burgeoning iron industry. The Caitlin & Saxton Company was the first to fit the building out for ironwork, making augers (drills) and bits for only a short time before it was put to use by Groome & Shattuck, wrench makers. The Eagle Mill even had a short stint in the clothing trade under Paul Smith's leadership but was soon back to iron products under Joseph Allen.

Joseph Allen worked in an auger factory as a young boy in Connecticut, where he learned the trade before he was seventeen. He then purchased a quantity of clocks, which he traded for thirty-two horses, hoping to sell them in the Caribbean, but the ship was wrecked and he was ruined. Allen found a creditor and his next shipment of horses paid both debts and left him a profit. He then returned to the auger factory until the fall of 1843, when he settled in Troy and entered into a partnership making augers with O.W. Edson. In 1846, Edson built his own auger factory on the lower Poesten Kill at Troy, and in later years he entered the cuff and collar business under the name Bennett & Edson, where he was one of the first to use sewing machines in cuff and collar making in 1855 (later he powered them by steam). Meanwhile, Joseph Allen had taken over the old auger factory in Troy and operated it on his own until it was destroyed by fire in 1850.

In January 1851, Allen purchased the Eagle Mill and fitted it out for high-volume production of augers, and in 1859 he added machinery for making hoes for the southern market. Two years later, Allen closed the factory and enlisted to fight in the Civil War. He was wounded at the Battle of Cold Harbor and twice while leading a brigade at Fort Fisher and was appointed brevet lieutenant colonel by Abraham Lincoln. At the end of the war, Joseph Allen returned to Eagle Mills and joined with George T. Lane in producing cable chains, files and hoes, but afterward he settled into the making of hoes exclusively. In 1900, the Eagle Mill, then called the Planters Hoe Factory, employed thirteen men. Through several owners, the company lasted until 1907, and the building was destroyed in 1911 when a fire swept through the village, taking with it at least fifteen buildings. The upper Poesten Kill and Quacken Kill villages took part in other sectors of the iron industry as well. Hiram Phillips operated a foundry for making plows and other farm tools in Eagle Mills in the 1860s and 1870s. Other foundry owners included Henry Chichester and Henry Rowe.

Just as it had in Troy, water power in the villages on the upper Poesten Kill provided for the production of a wide variety of products. At Rock Hollow, east of Cropseyville on the Quacken Kill, there was a paper mill operated by Howland Gardener (a founder of Manning Paper) and a wood turning factory operated by Salmon Daniels. The Daniels factory made the woodenwares, including brush blocks and handles, for the brush factories in

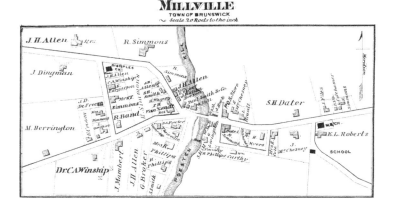

Eagle Mills, once known as Millville, was home to a variety of manufactories. A hoe factory, gristmill, wagon maker, foundry and sawmill are all shown here. *Courtesy Poestenkill Historical Society.*

Lansingburgh. In the 1860s, Hamilton B. Lawton began making carpet warp and twine in Rock Hollow, and in the 1860s Poestenkill was home to two carriage factories, a stove-facing factory and a factory making mowing machines. In 1877, H.C. Hoag established a factory in the village to make Excelsior Hay Rakes. The largest manufacturer in Poestenkill Village was located beside the Poesten Kill on the east side of Farm-to-Market Road. Power was supplied by an underground raceway that fed an overshot wheel providing eight horsepower. Like the Eagle Mill downstream, the building was used by a number of proprietors making a variety of goods; inside was a small iron forge.

The building was a carriage shop before wheelwright and wagon builder Lawton B. Hoag established his business there by the early 1850s. Lawton's sons William, John and Harrison also learned the carriage building trade there, and in 1871 they advertised that they were a "manufacturer of sleighs, both heavy and light. Repairing, Carriage Ironing and Painting in all its branches promptly attended to." In the 1860s, William Hoag partnered with tanner Nicholas Taylor to form a cotton batten factory on the building's second floor. In a cotton batten factory, after the longest fibers of the cotton have been made into cloth, the short fiber byproducts are pressed into cotton batten, a soft cotton mat used in coverlets, comforters, cushions and pillows. The Hoag & Taylor operation was not the first (Poestenkill had both a fulling mill and batten factory as early as 1840) but it was the most successful. In 1875, the men had $1,500 in real estate and $1,200 in tools and machinery invested, they owned fifteen tons of cotton valued at $3,000 and with four men annually produced about four tons of batten. In the 1880s, muslin and linen shirts were made on the second-floor facility that was then run by John H. Dater. Dater supplied Troy, Chatham and merchants in the surrounding towns, and also local townsfolk, whose names are recorded in his account books. Lucien Wager, whose father Aaron also had a wagon shop nearby and who had married one of William Hoag's daughters, later operated the wagon shop and expanded the second-floor factory to eventually produce lace-trimmed corset covers. About 1940, the building was converted into a garage owned by Walter Forebellar; it was demolished to make way for the widening of the highway.

Cropseyville had larger textile mills. In 1866, the old Cropsey gristmill was acquired by Reuben Smith. Reuben's son Paul Smith, who also operated a sawmill, improved the works, and in 1890 the Smith mill shipped sixty-two thousand bushels of corn, oats, buckwheat and rye flour to New York City. Smith also established a shirt factory at Cropseyville in 1882. At first business was good, but as domestic competition increased and the price of shirts dropped, Smith reported that his business fell off considerably. From 1891 through 1893, for instance, the Smith factory did not run full time. At the mill's height, Smith employed seventy-five people, mostly women, a considerable workforce for the little hamlet, and sold his shirts via salesmen throughout the country. His workers earned between five and eleven dollars per fifty-nine-hour workweek, and many lived in a boardinghouse down the street (formerly Valentine Cropsey's Hall). By 1897, however, the Smith factory was in decline and employed only twenty women; in 1900 just five were employed. The Smith mill was forced into bankruptcy and was acquired by Herman Brust before it was demolished about 1950.

Leonard Lynd built this farmhouse on the Poesten Kill in Poestenkill Village and his son Edgar installed the "Tank House Shop," a three-story collar factory. A windmill pumped water into a large water tank on the top floor, which powered sewing machines below operated by about a dozen women and girls. *Courtesy Poestenkill Historical Society.*

Another family of mill owners in Cropseyville were the Greens, who occupied a mill on South Road at a dam and millpond near what is now Fred's Falls (built by Walter D. McChesney about 1790). Before 1855, Franklin and Orlando J. Green also operated a wool carding mill where clean wool was fed into carding machines, essentially revolving cylinders, each covered with fine teeth. Revolving in opposite directions, the wool fibers were drawn apart, resulting in a thin, flat sheet. The sheet was then condensed into a rope called roving, which could be wound on large spools or bobbins and spun into yarn in a spinning mill before being woven into cloth. In 1886, the Green Mill also included fulling facilities where rough wool cloth was matted or felted by applying pressure, moisture and heat in order to give the cloth greater strength. Workers in fulling mills saturated the cloth with soap and hot water and passed it between slowly turning rollers. Two years later, the mills were described as making cashmeres, flannels and yarns and having four looms. After the death of Orlando Green in 1891, Franklin continued the operations with his son, Albert A. Greene. The textile mill was destroyed by fire in 1901, but Albert continued with the milling of flour and feed, and that mill is still standing, possibly the only surviving building from the heyday of water power on the Quacken Kill.

As the industries in the villages of both Poestenkill and Eagle Mills waned in the latter 1800s, garden farming was on the rise, supplying those who did not live on farms with the needed delivery of hay, milk, eggs and other dairy products such as butter and cheese. The farmers along the Poesten Kill's upper reaches in the towns of Brunswick and Poestenkill were more than happy to supply their needs, and many established delivery routes into Troy along with local creameries. Farms like the Dater Farm on Brunswick Road in Eagle Mills took great advantage of market farming in the nineteenth and twentieth centuries. In 1919, A.B. Jones's thirty-two-acre farm on the Quacken Kill in Cropseyville was growing apples, pears, cherries, plums, grapes, strawberries, raspberries, hay and grain but was "best suited to potatoes."

Another development rose from the emergence of the turnpikes as major routes into the mountains of eastern Rensselaer County. With improved roads and more traffic, a number of locals went into a variety of tourist businesses, particularly along Routes 2 and 7. Tourist homes (bed-and-breakfasts, inns), family restaurants and a variety of tourist attractions encouraged travelers to stop along the road. Eagle Mills included homes with names like Breezy Meadows, Sweet's and the Friendly Door that were opened to tourists. Homes in Poestenkill were also let to tourist as well. Around 1900, for instance, Mrs. E.E. Lynd was advertising her home Lyndwood: "Country residence; all modern improvements; shady lawns, spacious verandas; table and service excellent; own vegetables; terms moderate." Locals also established roadside stands selling soft drinks, candy, ice cream and homemade souvenirs. The Fremonts, and later the Bentleys, kept a caged bear at Clum's Corners to attract visitors to their roadside stand. Another stand was located at the first bridge over the Poesten Kill (White Bridge) outside Troy, where the Shippey family ran a snack bar for those who swam and fished in the kill nearby.

The Poesten Kill at low water in Barberville, site of a popular roadside hotel in the 1800s. Visitors taking in the natural scenery of the Poesten Kill provided needed income to the businesses along what was once an important turnpike to Berlin. *Courtesy Poestenkill Historical Society.*

By the second half of the 1800s, poorly situated trade centers declined in prosperity as economic conditions changed. Villages like Eagle Mills, Cropseyville, Poestenkill and East Poestenkill survived but were far from the bustling local places they had been in the first several decades of the 1800s. Gradually, the westward movement of the fur and lumber frontiers reduced the need for the tanneries and lumber mills; imported flour and feed reduced local demand for gristmilling services; and colliers no longer plied the streets in large numbers with charcoal, their product being replaced by imported coal. In 1886, there were about a dozen coal dealers in Troy. One of them, Tom S. Wotkyns, had storage capacity for nine thousand tons of coal.

WORKERS

South Troy and the Irish

The water power of the Poesten Kill magnified the amount of production that could be accomplished by mechanics working with their hands and work animals. As harnessing the natural power of the kill expanded, more equipment necessitated the need for more skilled workers. Designers, builders and installers of machinery were in demand, as were those who maintained and inspected equipment and eventually those who watched over the operation and its employees and managed its sales, accounting and capital needs. Few people were needed to run the small grist- and sawmills of the 1600s and 1700s, but increasingly complex machinery and higher production along the Poesten Kill required a diversified workforce in the 1800s.

Before about 1830, the largest companies on the lower kill employed fewer than 100 workers. Most of the firms were small, primarily local companies supplying local markets. Over the next thirty years, however, the lower Poesten Kill exploded into a large industrial zone of companies producing a wide variety of products and sometimes employing thousands of workers, and the outlying towns of Poestenkill and Brunswick also saw some industrial growth. Much of this growth was spurred by technological changes in the textile and iron industries, improvements in transportation, the opening of new markets in the West (and overseas) and the widening regional industrial base itself. The population of Troy grew from about 11,500 in 1830 to nearly 40,000 by 1860. By 1860, Troy's factories employed more than 10,000 workers. Iron and iron products were the second largest industry, employing about 2,000 people, next to the cotton, textiles, clothing and garments industries, which employed about 7,000. In the 1880s, the Burden Iron Company on its own was producing almost one million horseshoes a week, and about 5,000 people worked in South Troy's iron and steel industries.

Initially, many of those settling into jobs at the Poesten Kill mills and factories were skilled mechanics from New England and the mid-Atlantic or were emigrants from England and Scotland. Before 1845, there were few Irish (and fewer African Americans), but in the ten years that followed Irish immigrants fleeing the famine moved into the mills along the Poesten Kill in large numbers. So many Irish immigrants arrived in Troy in the years 1845 through 1848 that temporary sheds were built to house them and keep them isolated from the rest of the population out of fear that they might bring contagious diseases. With the influx of Irish, the population of Ida Hill more than doubled and its foreign-born population grew to nearly 40 percent, almost 30 percent of them foreign-born Irish. They generally served in the unskilled positions of the mills and factories, in shops and public services. They lived in some of the cheapest housing in Troy, thanks in part to the series of fires downtown that destroyed some nine hundred buildings and perhaps an equal number of outbuildings between 1820 and 1862. After the fire of 1854, which nearly overtook the mills on the lower Poesten Kill, the city began requiring more brick and stone construction. As a result, many from the poorer quarters increasingly found cheaper housing on Ida Hill and south of the Poesten Kill, where the vast majority of buildings were made of wood—far more than any of the city's other wards into the 1870s. By 1890, the Ida Hill neighborhood was the second most populated ward in the entire city and composed 10 percent of Troy's total population (it had been the smallest ward in 1845).

About the same time as the growth of Ida Hill occurred, the city of Troy pressed south over the Poesten Kill, creating a mixed but largely Irish immigrant community in South Troy. Until the late 1800s, the area around the Poesten Kill was largely industrial, although a small number of local retail shops and residences (including a number of tenements, apartments and boardinghouses) were scattered among the various manufacturing facilities. Unlike in other mill towns in the area (such as Cohoes), workers in Troy were not generally confined to row housing, with the exception of those at Ida Terrace and in Hoboken Hollow on the hillside south of the Poesten Kill. The workers in Troy often constructed housing for themselves in the cheaper rent districts below the Poesten Kill and on Ida Hill.

Throughout the 1840s and 1850s, South Troy (as the area below the Poesten Kill was known) was increasingly left out of quality of life ordinances that applied to other parts of the city. For instance, in 1840 the Troy Common Council passed an ordinance forbidding (without special permission) the building of polluting industries—furnaces, steam planning machines, steam engines, blacksmith shops, smokehouses and the like—in the city, except in the Fifth Ward (Ida Hill and Albia) and the area south of the Poesten Kill. The ordinance was extended to include slaughterhouses in 1849 and varnish factories in 1864. When the common council passed an ordinance to ensure the lighting and maintenance of gas streetlamps, it only applied to the area north of the Poesten Kill. When telephone, telegraph and electrical lines were required to be removed and put into underground conduits about 1900, the area below State Street was exempted, which explains why the lines still stand in South Troy.

The concentration of industrial operations south of the Poesten Kill tended to exclude even churches, schools and social service institutions from the South End (aside from the Mechanics Hall on Mill Street at the intersection with Spring Avenue). Although there was an area of intensive social services centered on St. Mary's Church that had grown at the base of Mount Ida north of the Poesten Kill, in the late 1800s there were few churches serving the area around the lower Poesten Kill. Between Washington Park and the Poesten Kill there were just two: Saint Jean Baptiste (St. John the Baptist) and St. Laurence; south of the Poesten Kill there was only St. Joseph's. Saint Jean Baptiste was a French-speaking congregation that was organized in 1850 on Ferry Street; its church on Second Street, south of Adams, was dedicated in 1869.

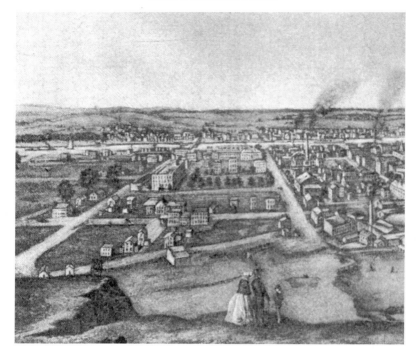

This detail of an 1840s view from Mount Ida shows that residential development took some time to make its way south to the Poesten Kill. *Courtesy Troy Public Library.*

St. Laurence's Church was a German-speaking Roman Catholic congregation. It was first organized at meetings at St. Mary's Church and then for a year at Alexander Lutzelberger's Billiard Hall on River Street; its members met at the French church in 1869 and the following year began building their church on the southeast corner of Third and Jefferson Streets.

Four blocks south stood one of the only churches south of the Poesten Kill, St. Joseph's on Jackson Street, between Third and Fourth Streets. Known as the "iron workers' church," St. Joseph's was also the city's Irish church. Reverend Peter Havermans (pastor of St. Mary's Church and Troy's first and most prominent Roman Catholic Church leader) helped secure eight lots and the cornerstone was laid in May 1847. That same month, men from the Burden Works dug the church's foundation. In February 1848, however, the original plans for St. Joseph's had to be changed in order to save money for the diocese, which needed additional funds for the cathedral in Albany and to rebuild St. Peter's Church, which had been recently destroyed by fire. The changes were made and on November 1 the first Mass was celebrated by Havermans in the still unfinished church. Six years later, the church was finally finished at a cost of $100,000; it sat two thousand people and featured Tiffany windows, a marble altar, mahogany pews, a baptistery, an organ and choir loft and a bell tower.

As a gathering place for Irish immigrants, the church became a symbol for their community. Church-sponsored social events and organizations helped the parishioners become aquianted with their new homes, particularly on St. Patrick's Day, when parades and special Masses were held. Irish music and the Irish language were often heard at these events and even in the parish school, established in 1861 to deal with the "unruly youth of South Troy." In 1868, a new convent at the head of Jackson Street on Fourth was built, and St. Joseph's Academy was built in 1876, one of the school buildings facing Third Street and the other Monroe. A private girls' school was operated until 1883, and a high school was maintained until the establishment of Catholic Central High School (now West Hall on the RPI campus) in 1924. In 1957, a grade school was opened at the corner of Fourth and Monroe Streets. Additional buildings on the sprawling campus included a large parish hall built in 1897 that housed an auditorium, a gymnasium and four bowling lanes. A maternity hospital was built east of the church on Fourth Street in 1923 but closed in 1952 and served as the convent until 1963.

The Irish made up the most significant immigrant population along the lower Poesten Kill in the second half of the 1800s. They were active in the local labor movement; Kate Mullaney organized the first all-female labor union in the Untied States, the Troy Collar Laundry Union, in the 1860s. The Irish Republican movement in Troy was strong. Some one hundred Troy Irish marched north to join the Fenian invasion of Canada in 1866, and that fall the Fenian National Congress was held in the city. In 1903, Irish labor leader and later Easter Rising martyr James Connolly organized workers in Troy. Irish workers of all stripes rose through the police, fire and political ranks, among them the Irish folk hero, gangster, gambler, boxer, politician and founder of the Saratoga thoroughbred track, John "Old Smoke" Morrissey. *Representative Young Irish-Americans of Troy, NY*, published in 1889, includes portraits and biographies of some one hundred prominent Troy Irishmen, many of them members of local unions (particularly the molders' union), policemen, politicians and members of the Robert Emmet Association and the Pilsner Democratic Club. One of them was Dennis J. Whelan, who was born in Ireland in 1846 and was brought to Troy at the age of four. After returning from the Civil War, Whelan began making soda water and "other temperance drinks" on Jefferson Street, less than a block from the Poesten Kill in a building that still stands. In 1880, he was elected alderman from the Eleventh Ward (along the south side of the kill) for a short term and was reelected again that fall. In 1882, he was made president of the common council and served in that capacity until 1886, when he was chosen mayor. In 1889, Whalen oversaw the sale of the city's remaining lots south of the Poesten Kill. He had two new firehouses built below the Poesten Kill and a large school built on Pawling Avenue.

Recently, another immigrant neighborhood took its place in the history of Troy. The Little Italy neighborhood, which stretched from Fourth Street to Hill Street and from Ferry to the Poesten Kill, still retains much of its late 1800s character. Although the Troy Urban Renewal Agency began demolishing much of the central downtown business area in 1966 and the opening of the Troy Plaza on Hoosick Street the following year siphoned retail business from downtown, city residents, particularly north of the Poesten Kill, have been organizing to bring their neighborhoods back to life. Local business owners, residents and the city are partnering to highlight the Little Italy and Pottery District neighborhoods' walkable historic appeal. Commercial buildings are being adapted for reuse and residences are being restored, breathing new life into the lower stretches of one of the county's most important waterways.

WORKERS AND
INDUSTRIAL PROTEST

The Mariners' Benevolent Association was formed in Troy in 1830 for the mutual welfare and relief of its members. Probably not a union in today's sense, the association was the forerunner of later organized labor organizations that took improvement of working conditions as a significant goal. That same year, a Farmers', Mechanics' and Workingmen's Party was organized in Troy, and in 1842 the first local strike occurred at Harmony Mills in Cohoes when workers walked out after their wages were cut by 20 percent. The millworkers in Cohoes battled the owners over wages throughout 1857 and into 1858, and the Harmony Mills workers won a 12 percent wage increase, the first such victory in the textile mills. On the heels of the labor victory in Cohoes, six men formed the Iron Molders' International Union No. 2 in Troy in April 1858. Within a week, the union expanded to fifty-one members and elected Simon F. Mann president. In 1859, a strike of the Troy ironworkers won them the right to regulate the workforce. By 1860, Local No. 2 had become the largest local in the country, with some four hundred members. Workers also organized in the collar industry. In 1864, labor activist Kate Mullaney organized the first all-female labor union in the United States, the Troy Collar Laundry Union, composed of the city's collar laundresses. After its formation, the union struck and won a 25 percent increase in wages.

The latter years of the Civil War were marked by great progress in Troy's unions. In 1864 alone, in addition to the victory of the

Collar Laundry Union, the iron molders struck and won a 15 percent increase in wages, the Troy Trades' Assembly was organized with fourteen local unions and the Workingmen's Cooperative Association opened a cooperative grocery for workers. In 1865, the Workingmen's Eight-Hour League was formed to advocate for the eight-hour day, and at a convention in Albany the Trades Assembly of New York State, the first state labor federation in the nation, was organized. In April of that year, about seven thousand workers held a mass meeting to oppose the anti-labor Hastings Bill, and in July a Workingmen's Free Reading Room and Library was established. In November, a Laborers' Union was organized with one hundred members—within a year it had five hundred. In 1866, the first regular issue of the *Saturday Evening Herald*, a Troy labor paper, was published (no copies are known to exist). The *Clarion*, a paper published by the Knights of Labor, was circulated in Troy beginning in 1886.

The successful organizing of the Civil War period led to the largest industrial protest in Troy history—the Great Lockout of Troy Iron Molders. It began on March 17, 1866, when Troy's foundry owners locked out about 750 iron molders in an attempt to break the union. The result was a sympathy strike of the pattern makers and stove mounters and the construction of a cooperative stove foundry at the corner of River Street and Glen Avenue in North Troy. After two months, the strike was ended when the Clinton Stove Works agreed to the union's terms. The female workers of Troy didn't fare as well, though. In 1868, the laundress union struck and organized its own cooperative, but after three months the strike was broken and the union collapsed after the collar and cuff makers started producing products made of paper. The cooperative was soon out of business. The good news for female workers in Troy was that one of their leaders, Kate Mullaney, became the first woman to hold a national union position when she was appointed assistant secretary of the National Labor Union. The following year, female workers in Troy's typographical and laundry unions were finally admitted to the New York State Workingmen's Assembly in Albany.

Labor activism continued in the 1870s, mostly among the iron- and steel workers. Members of Empire Forge of the Sons of Vulcan walked out of the Bessemer plant in January 1873, and in June the puddlers at the Burden nail factory struck and were locked out until December, when an agreement was reached following the plant's being shut down. Within a year, the Sons of Vulcan struck again rather than accept a wage reduction. This time the heaters joined the strike and Troy's iron and steel mills were forced to close for the duration of the thirty-one-week strike. That strike was marked by violence on both sides, precipitating what has been called Troy's "reign of terror" against nonunion replacement workers during strikes from 1875 to 1877. Many of the problems arose when the stove founders announced wage decreases between 10 and 30 percent and several announced that they would reopen immediately using nonunion labor. In 1877, the stove founders negotiated contracts for prison labor and violence against nonunion molders increased. Among the most serious incidents were a suspected arson at the Clinton Foundry and the large crowds who intimidated nonunion workers outside the foundries. The worst of the troubles came to an end when the union conceded to the founders in order to regain their jobs in June 1877, just in time for the nationwide railroad strikes and violence that precipitated the calling out of the National Guard.

The 1880s were a mixed time for organized labor along the Poesten Kill and throughout Troy, with wider political advances countered by local defeats. A Workingmen's Trade Assembly (later the Central Federation of Labor) and the first Knights of Labor association were formed in Troy in 1882 (by 1886 there were thirty chapters), the same year that New York governor David B. Hill proclaimed the first Labor Day. In 1885, contract prison labor was abolished in New York State. The ironworkers in Troy didn't fare well, however, and the most disastrous strike occurred on Ida Hill. In February 1883, the Malleable Iron Company on the north side of Congress Street locked out its workers (about ninety) who were members of Troy Molders Union, replacing the men with nonunion workers. The ensuing struggle was marked by serious violence, including beatings and threats of death, shootings by both sides and numerous charges of arson. Thirty-three of the nonunion men lived at the St. Francis boardinghouse on Fifteenth Street on Ida

Women were a large part of the workforce along the Poesten Kill. In the 1880s, muslin and linen shirts were made by women in this small factory

above a wagon shop on a raceway in Poestenkill Village. *Courtesy Poestenkill Historical Society.*

Hill and were protected by city police along with private gunmen hired by the company.

Throughout the spring of 1883, the two sides became more entrenched and more hostile. The conflict spilled into violence on June 9, when several shots were fired at striking workers from the nonunion boardinghouse. The next day, several nonunion men paraded in front of Mehan's, a bar on Congress Street where the union men were meeting. The following day, they showed up again, and this time a fight ensued and several nonunion men drew guns and began shooting. William Hutchison, a union molder employed in the city's cooperative foundry, was shot in the chest. Joseph Wineston, another union man, was shot in the mouth and Arthur Imeson was shot twice in the leg. When police arrived, the shooting was still going on. They rushed in and arrested Sanford C. White and Thomas Canfield for the gun play but a crowd soon gathered looking to lynch White. In the melee that followed, several policemen were roughed up by the crowd but White was saved from the mob.

Hutchison's funeral the next day was attended by several thousand people, including members of the Albany Molders Union and other Troy unions that supported the strike. Not to be surpassed by their "comrades" in Troy, the Knights of Labor in Brockville, Ontario, held an even larger funeral when the Troy molders brought his body home. The funeral was described as the largest cortège ever seen in Brockville. The case became known as the Ida Hill Murder and the proprietor of the works, William Sleicher, the brother of *Leslie's Weekly* publisher John A. Sleicher and a director of the National State Bank of Troy, was arrested for murder (the charges did not hold). In the meantime, some union molders infiltrated the Malleable Iron Company works and in December won a tremendous victory when all but four of the ninety-some nonunion men joined the union. The owners responded by hiring nonunion German immigrants, and the strike was finally ended after sixteen months when the molders were forced to accept a 20 percent wage reduction.

The 1890s were relatively quiet, but for the more than twenty years beginning in 1900 it was the turn of the streetcar motormen and conductors. Strikes were started in 1900, but the first significant walkout began on May 7, 1901, with five hundred Albany streetcar workers of the United Traction Company. They were joined by one hundred ship workers and four hundred Troy trolley workers. The strikers sought union recognition, a raise in pay and protections from arbitrary punishments. On the night of May 15, the company's tracks crossing the Poesten Kill on the Red Bridge at Fourth Street were torn up and the rails were thrown into the kill. The following day, strikers began distributing white ribbons printed with the words "while the strike lasts we will walk." Ultimately the strike was unsuccessful. Additional strikes against the company occurred in 1918 and in 1921, but by then the age of the trolley was coming to an end.

FLOODS ALONG THE
POESTEN KILL

Floods were a frequent occurrence along the Poesten Kill, as spring runoff annually flooded low-lying fields and the threat of ice dams was ever present. Aside from flooding, drought could also affect the operation of the mills. Major flooding occurred along the Poesten Kill, or on the Hudson at the mouth of the kill, in 1852, 1857 (highest flood ever recorded at Albany, almost twenty-two feet), 1869, 1871, 1874 (when a portion of the Congress Street bridge fell in), 1890, 1891, 1913 (which did a great amount of damage along the Poesten Kill in Troy), 1914, 1918, 1922, 1927, 1936, 1938 (which damaged the mills on the lower Poesten Kill), 1948, 1949, 1955 and 1977.

About 2:00 a.m. on September 18, 1890, the dam at the outlet of Bonesteel Pond in East Poestenkill gave way "and water rushed down through the narrow valley, tearing up trees and carrying away everything standing in its course." According to the *New York Times*, six bridges were destroyed, along with three sawmills and the barns and shed of George Cottrell. At the hamlet of Barberville, John Randall's shoe shop was demolished but the water spread out along the flats there, saving the rest of the hamlet from destruction. At the village of Poestenkill, the streets were flooded and Wheeler's shoe shop was washed from its foundation. In Troy, the water "rose alarmingly" but did not flood its banks, even though Bonesteel Pond was completely drained of its water.

John Randall rebuilt his shoe shop at Barberville but less than a year later it was washed away again, this time in a much more

Floods along the Poesten Kill

Spring runoff annually flooded low-lying fields, and the threat of ice dams was ever present along the Poesten Kill. Major flooding has occurred along the Poesten Kill perhaps two dozen times since the kill was settled. This photo was taken at Poestenkill Village. *Courtesy Poestenkill Historical Society.*

destructive storm. It began the day before when a heavy rain swelled both the Poesten and Wynants Kills. Already the locals were worried, and the next day, when news of a large storm was received, "several men immediately mounted horses and proceeded to the farm houses on the banks of the creek and gave the alarm." By 7:00 p.m., the water had risen considerably and carried away several bridges and sluices, including the iron bridge near Hammond Herrington's in East Poestenkill. "Mr. Herrington's large flats are entirely submerged," the *New York Times* reported the next day, "completely destroying a large crop of potatoes and almost ruining the flats. A barn occupied by Porter Herrington, who lives in the house, was carried away. The roads are all gullied or washed out so as to be almost impassable, especially on the hills."

Below Barberville, one of the residents who received a warning of the coming flood was Nelson Barringer, who immediately drove his cows from the barn to high ground. His family soon followed, wading through the high water to reach safety. Others were not so lucky though, and four people were swept away when floodwaters destroyed the village bridge on which they were standing. Garret Ives had just been standing on the bridge with his wife Alice but had gone back to the house on some chore, leaving her behind

The Poesten Kill is about to flood its banks in Barberville at a spot that flooded twice in two years (1890 and 1891), damaging John Randall's shoe shop both times. *Courtesy Poestenkill Historical Society.*

Floods along the Poesten Kill

Remains of the destroyed bridge in Poestenkill Village, probably during the flood of 1922. This bridge was also damaged in the flooding of 1891 and 1938. *Courtesy Poestenkill Historical Society.*

to watch the high water. At that moment, the bridge was washed away and Alice, along with William McChesney, William Castler and Robert Morrison, was swept into the raging torrent. Alice and Morrison were pulled from the creek alive but McChesney was drowned. According to the August 28, 1891 *Troy Times*, "Castler was taken down the Poestenkill about a mile and the next morning was found at the top of a tree where he had passed the night." As bad as it was on the Poesten Kill, those along the Wynants Kill fared worse. Dozens of homes and businesses were destroyed.

A look at the bridge on Farm-to-Market Road in Poestenkill Village shows the constant struggle of those along the Poesten Kill to keep the roads across the kill open. The bridge was destroyed in the flooding of 1891 and was rebuilt as an iron truss bridge. During the flood of 1922, one end of the bridge fell from its pier and was again replaced, this time with a steel girder bridge. The 1922 bridge was destroyed when the main center pier gave way during one of the most destructive flooding events along the Poesten Kill—the Great New England Hurricane—in October 1938. The storm hit Long Island (where it got another popular name, the Long Island

The bridge at Barberville was knocked from its piers during the Great New England Hurricane of 1938, which also left many of the mill buildings along the north side of the lower Poesten Kill beyond repair. *Courtesy Poestenkill Historical Society.*

Express) as a Category 3 on September 21 and killed nearly seven hundred people, damaged or destroyed over 57,000 homes, knocked down a quarter million telephone poles and caused property losses estimated at $5 billion in today's dollars. Along the railroad line from Troy to Mechanicville, the storm damaged or destroyed five bridges and damaged the tracks at fifty places. The water in the Hudson crested at more than seventeen feet, and along the lower Poesten Kill many of the mills that remained along the north side were damaged beyond repair. The flooding of 1938 finished what was left of the mills on the lower Poesten Kill—what nature had supplied, it had finally taken away.

BIBLIOGRAPHY

Anderson, George Baker. *Landmarks of Rensselaer County, New York.* Syracuse, NY: D. Mason & Co., 1897.

Bliven, Rachel D., Robert N. Andersen, G. Steven Draper, Eva Gemmill, Hughes Gemmill, Joseph A. Parker and Helen M. Upton. *A Resourceful People: A Pictorial History of Rensselaer County, New York.* Norfolk, VA: Donning Co., 1987.

Bradley, James W. *Before Albany: An Archaeology of Native-Dutch Relations in the Capital Region 1600–1664.* Albany: New York State Education Department, 2007.

Dunn, Shirley W. *The Mohicans and Their Lands: 1609–1730.* Fleischmanns, NY: Purple Mountain Press, 1994.

Groft, Tammis K. *Cast with Style: Nineteenth Century Cast-Iron Stoves from the Albany Area.* Albany, NY: Albany Institute of History and Art, 1984.

Hill, Florence M. *West of Perigo: Poestenkill Memories.* Troy, NY: Whitehurst Printing, 1979.

Howe, Edward. "The Hudson-Mohawk Region Industrializes: 1609–1860." *The Hudson River Valley Review* 19, no. 2 (September 2002).

BIBLIOGRAPHY

Lilly, Robert J. *The Wynants Kill: A Small Stream, But Mighty.* West Sand Lake, NY: aGatherin', 2005.

McClure Zeller, Nancy Anne, ed. *A Beautiful and Fruitful Place: Selected Rensselaerswjck Seminar Papers.* Albany, NY: New Netherland Publishing, 1991.

Pearson, Jonathan, et al. *A History of the Schenectady Patent in the Dutch and English Times; being contributions toward a history of the lower Mohawk Valley.* Edited by J.W. MacMurray. Albany, NY: J. Munsell's Sons, Printers, 1883.

Phelan, Thomas, and P. Thomas Carroll. *Hudson Mohawk Gateway: An Illustrated History.* Sun Valley, CA: American Historical Press, 2001.

Renolds, Cuyler, ed. *Hudson-Mohawk Genealogical and Family Memoirs, Vol. II.* New York: Lewis Historical Publishing Company, 1911.

Schmitt, Claire K. *Natural Areas of Rensselaer County New York.* Schenectady, NY: Capital Printing, 1994.

Schumacher, Murial. "Manufacturing & Industry in Rensselaerwyck." *Dutch Settler Society of Albany Yearbook 38.* Albany, NY: Dutch Settler Society, 1962–63.

Sylvester, Nathaniel Bartlett. *History of Rensselaer Co., New York.* Philadelphia: Everts & Peck, 1880.

Thibadeau, Bart. "Troy's Poestenkill Gorge; A chapter in the continuing story of industrial man versus the limitations of his environment." *Intersections* 3, no. 2 (Fall 1976).

Van Laer, A.J.F., trans. and ed. *Van Rensselaer Bowier Manuscripts.* Albany: University of the State of New York, 1908.

BIBLIOGRAPHY

Venema, Janny. *Beverwijck: A Dutch Village on the American Frontier, 1652–1664.* Albany: State of New York University Press, 2003.

Weise, Arthur James. *The City of Troy and Its Vicinity.* Troy, NY: E. Green, 1886.

————. *History of the City of Troy, From the Expulsion of the Mohegan Indians to the Present Centennial Year of the Independence of the United States of America.* Troy, NY: William H. Young, 1876.

Visit us at
www.historypress.net